Exploring the Oregon Coast

By William L. Mainwaring

Westridge Press
1090 Southridge, Pl. S
Salem, Oregon 97302

Acknowledgments

Many knowledgeable Oregonians have contributed valuable information or suggestions for this book, or have reviewed copy to prevent errors.

Officials of the State Parks and Recreation Branch and of the Travel Information Section of the Highway Division, and of the State Fish and Wildlife Department, have been particularly helpful.

Others making noteworthy contributions include editors of The Daily Astorian, The Newport News-Times, The Curry County Reporter and The Brookings-Harbor Pilot; Chamber of Commerce officials at Astoria, Seaside, Cannon Beach, Tillamook, Pacific City, Lincoln City, Toledo, Yachats, Florence, Lakeside, North Bend, Coos Bay, Bandon, Port Orford, Gold Beach and Brookings; Forest Service officials at Hebo, Waldport, Mapleton, Reedsport, Gold Beach, Brookings and Grants Pass; and the Tillamook County Planning Department.

The author is responsible for, and regrets, any errors. They would have been more numerous without the generous assistance of many individuals and organizations.

Credits

Design Consultant: Jac Crawford
Maps: Cynthia Mendelson
Typography: The Statesman-Journal Co.
Color Separations: Pacific Color Plate Co.
Lithography: Universal Color

Photographs

Most of the photographs were taken by the author. Wally Blackburn of Gold Beach took the pictures of the Rogue River on pages 54 and 55 (bottom.) Sea Lion Caves, Inc., supplied the photo on page 40. The Travel Information Section of the State Highway Division provided the following photographs: page 8, top and bottom; page 9, bottom; page 11, top; page 20, top and bottom; page 26; page 28, top; page 33, top; page 51, top; page 55, top; page 62, top.

Second Printing: March, 1981

Photographs:

Cover: Heceta Head Lighthouse
Right: Near Hug Point State Park
Page 4: View from Cape Perpetua

Contents

Exploring the Oregon Coast

Introduction

I want you, the reader, to discover and enjoy everything the magnificent Oregon Coast has to offer.

This book points out hundreds of fascinating things to see and do along the Oregon Coast, from Astoria to Brookings. I hope you will find it a useful guide for fun and travel, one that helps you make the most of limited time, money and gasoline.

Oregon is blessed with a coastline of scenic beauty and variety unmatched on this continent. It's a delightful place, where the Pacific surf washes and sometimes pounds the western edge of our continent. It's a land of storms and sunburns, of wharves and lighthouses, of salt air and fading paint. It's a perfect place for the human psyche to unwind, for workaday tensions to be washed away by the rhythmic cadence of the surf.

Mighty headlands stand guard above the sea, from Tillamook Head south to Cape Ferrelo. Sandy beaches line much of the shore; some extend many miles to distant horizons, while others are nestled in secluded coves between protective promontories. Lush rain forests border the beaches along much of the northern coast, while farther south one finds the continent's most massive coastal sand dunes and the rugged, grass-covered bluffs of Curry County. Rivers great and small interrupt the coastline, including some that have carved out sizeable bays.

Varied activities here will provide endless enjoyment for you and your family.

The automobile is a practical tool for exploring the Oregon Coast. But you'll see and feel this marvelous land best if you cover much of it by foot, or by bicycle, boat or horseback. Delightful hiking trails have been developed in many places, including the northern portion of the Oregon Coast Trail, which eventually will be extended south to the California line. You'll want to walk along many beaches — to collect driftwood or shells or agates, perhaps, or to examine the exciting intertidal marine life, or simply to absorb the fascinating and relaxing atmosphere of the beach. You may want to sunbathe in the deep sand, build sand castles, or wade or swim in the chilling surf of the Pacific Ocean.

The temptations are endless for fishermen. Charter boats or private vessels will take you into the Pacific for salmon or a variety of other species. Numerous coastal streams are famous for their annual spawning runs of salmon, steelhead and cutthroat trout. Other anglers drop lines off rocks, docks and jetties, or cast off the beach. Freshwater lakes are tempting, too. And you can drop crab rings off boats or docks, or dig clams in the tide flats or along sandy beaches.

Plan some of your meals over campfires on the beach, and others at picnic tables with marvelous oceanfront views. You can find delicious fare at hundreds of places, ranging from simple seafood houses near the docks to gourmet restaurants. Similarly, the lodging ranges from attractive campgrounds to some of the nation's finest motels and condominiums.

A longtime Salem newspaperman, this is my first attempt at a book. I'm the author, primary photographer, editor and publisher. So, if the book misses the mark, it's pretty obvious who deserves the blame. After spending countless weekends and vacation weeks at the Oregon Coast for nearly 20 years, I thought I knew it fairly well. But this project led me into many fascinating areas I'd previously bypassed. Often accompanied by my wife, Mary, and our three children, I've had great fun exploring the Oregon Coast. Now I hope you'll get as much enjoyment from things I've described, and that you'll discover your own special treasures in this enchanting land beside the sea. — William L. Mainwaring

Sweeping view from atop the Astoria Column, across the city and down the Columbia River to the sea.

Historic Astoria

The first permanent white settlement in the Pacific Northwest, Astoria is a treasure trove of regional history.

It's also famous for the nationally-renowned salmon fishing of the lower Columbia River and nearby Pacific Ocean.

Our north-to-south tour of the Oregon Coast begins here, where the mighty Columbia concludes its 1,200-mile journey from Canada to the sea. The nation's third largest river drains a basin of 259,000 square miles, nearly the size of Texas.

If you arrive from the north, you'll cross the great river on the four-mile-long Astoria Interstate (toll) Bridge. Or perhaps you'll become better acquainted with the Columbia by driving down its south bank from Portland, through a series of picturesque river towns. If so, the $460 million Trojan nuclear power plant welcomes visitors Monday through Saturday from 9:30 to 5 and on Sundays from noon to 6 p.m.

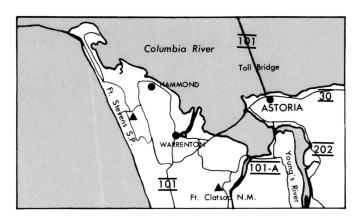

You also can tour the huge Crown Zellerbach paper mill at Wauna, on Tuesdays and Thursdays from June through September at 2:30 p.m.

After many other navigators had tried and failed, Capt. Robert Gray of Boston was the first white man to discover the great river of the West. He sailed his "Columbia" past Cape Disappointment and present Astoria in 1792, before turning back opposite Tongue Point. Then the historic Lewis and Clark Expedition followed the Columbia to the Pacific in late 1805. The hardy explorers spent that winter at nearby Fort Clatsop. Their reports of abundant sea otter persuaded John Jacob Astor to establish a fur trading post here in 1811. His men moored the "Tonquin" in deep water along the river's south bank. They constructed a stockade just up the hill, where later settlers would plat the intersection of 15th and Exchange Streets. But Astor's dreams of riches were dashed by the loss of supply ships, and the War of 1812 posed the threat of British capture. So in 1813 he sold Fort Astoria to a Canadian company, which moved its headquarters upriver to Fort Vancouver a dozen years later. But Astoria's strategic location continued to attract white settlers. When the Boundary Treaty of 1846 confirmed future U.S. control of the area, Astoria quickly acquired the first U.S. Post Office west of the Rocky Mountains.

Let's begin our Astoria visit by absorbing the region's marvelous physical setting from atop the Astoria Column. Follow the signs up Coxcomb Hill, in the southeast section of the city, to the lovely park at its 595-foot-high summit. It's crowned by the column, constructed in 1926 and modeled after one built by the Emperor Trajan in Rome. A handsome frieze spirals around the column's exterior, depicting major events in the region's history. Climb the 166 steps to the column's observation deck, if your health permits. There your eyes will be drawn northwest across the city, past Baker Bay and Cape Disappointment, to the mouth of the Columbia and beyond to the open sea (photo, page 6.) Turn to the east, looking up the river past Tongue Point to world — famous Mt. St. Helens. To the south, you'll gaze across Young's Bay and many miles of coastal forest to Saddle Mountain and Tillamook Head.

The Columbia River Maritime Musuem is another attraction you shouldn't miss. It houses one of the nation's finest collections of ship models and other fascinating nautical exhibits. The models range from early sailing vessels to modern freighters and warships. Note, for example, the replica of the U.S. Frigate "Constitution" ("Old Ironsides.") The "Inca" illustrates a five-masted schooner, typical of those which carried lumber from Astoria in the late 19th and early 20th centuries, before steamboats drove sailing ships from the high seas. An intricately detailed model of Astor's three-masted sailing ship "Tonquin" is a fine new acquisition. You'll also see navigation instruments, early sea charts, replicas of famous shipwrecks and lighthouse and fishing exhibits.

The museum is located at 16th and Exchange Streets (with plans to move to an imposing new structure in Astoria Maritime Park, probably in early 1981.) It's open daily from 10:30 to 5 p.m. from May through September, and daily except Monday from 10:30 to 4:30 p.m. from October through April. A modest admission fee is charged.

The museum's lightship "Columbia" (photo, page 7) may be toured during the same hours. Now berthed at Maritime Park at the foot of 17th Street, the "Columbia" stood guard off the mouth of the river for many years.

Astoria's prosperity during the latter 19th Century resulted in the construction of splendid homes by many of its leading families. Fortunately, some of these mansions have been preserved. They include Flavel House (photo, page 7), once described by an expert as the most beautiful example of Victorian architecture he had ever seen.

The heirs of Sea Captain George Flavel gave this showplace to the public. It's now the Clatsop County Museum, filled with interesting exhibits. Note its six fireplaces, all with hand-carved mantels and tiles imported from Italy and Holland. Handsome stairways with hand-turned hardwood railings lead upstairs. Climb to the fourth-floor cupola, where Flavel ob-

Flavel House, the Victorian mansion of an early sea captain, now houses the Clatsop County Museum.

Below: You can visit the lightship 'Columbia,' part of the superb Columbia River Maritime Museum.

Coffenbury Lake, above, and the rusting remains of the 'Peter Iredale,' below, are among the many popular attractions at Fort Stevens State Park, west of Astoria.

Below: The salmon fishing is great across the Columbia River bar, witness these gleaming silver salmon on a Warrenton dock.

served his ships in the harbor below. Located on 8th between Duane and Exchange Streets, it's open from 10 to 5 every day in summer, and from noon to 5 p.m. every day except Mondays between Sept. 15 and June 1. Modest contributions are encouraged.

You may want to view the exterior of other fine old Astoria homes. Drive to the corner of 17th and Grand and admire three mansions that date back to the 1879-1890 period. You'll find others, especially along Grand Avenue from 15th to 18th, and along Franklin Avenue from 8th to 13th. An Astoria Chamber of Commerce brochure lists addresses of interest.

Another historic attraction is the replica of Fort Astoria. An original bastion has been reconstructed at the site of the old fort, at 15th and Exchange streets. An adjoining mural depicts the stockade and other buildings.

The Astoria area is a mecca for sports fishermen as well as for history buffs. The Columbia River attracts the nation's richest salmon runs every spring, summer and fall. Sportsmen land an average of more than 450,000 salmon annually in the river or nearby ocean. Commercial fishermen catch another 750,000 or so, making this one of Oregon's leading commercial fishing centers.

Charter boats based in Warrenton, Hammond, Astoria and Ilwaco, Wash., take thousands of fishermen on all-day ocean trips from May to September. Many other private vessels moored at these ports also challenge the Columbia bar. When the seas are heavy, boats can pitch and roll on the ocean swells for several miles across the perilous bar, a place where numerous vessels have capsized over the years and hundreds of lives have been lost.

Others fish inside the bar, except during the river's closed season from April 1 to July 31. There's fine angling there for sea-run cutthroat in the fall and for steelhead through the winter.

One of Oregon's largest and most popular state parks covers part of the peninsula that reaches up to the river's south jetty, 10 miles west of Astoria.

Fort Stevens State Park has more than 600 campsites, 132 picnic tables, several lakes, a fine beach, many miles of hiking and bicycle trails, and interesting remnants of military fortifications.

Coffenbury Lake (photo, page 8) has two protected swimming beaches with bathhouses, a picnic area, a 2½-mile trail around the lake, boating, and fishing for trout and perch. Nearby Crabapple and Creep and Crawl Lakes also have boat ramps and fishing. The state's largest campground offers 260 tent sites, 120 improved (water and electricity) sites, and 223 trailer spaces with full utilities. It's open year-round; for reservations from mid-May through Labor Day, mail your request and $4 advance deposit check to the park at Hammond, Ore. 97121.

Drive west to the beach, where you'll see the surf licking at the remains of the "Peter Iredale." The once-proud 287-foot-long English four-masted bark was driven into the breakers and onto the beach by a 1906 winter storm. The crew was rescued, but the vessel was damaged beyond repair. Her skeleton has been rusting in the surf and gradually disintegrating ever since (photo, page 8). Razor clams are abundant on this beach; dig them on outgoing minus tides, except during the July 15-Aug. 31 closed season. It's also possible to drive down this beach at low tide, south 10 miles to Gearhart. Avoid soft sand and wet spots.

You can see remains of the army fort that was constructed here during the Civil War, to guard the mouth of the river from Confederate or foreign gunboats. The military abandoned Fort Stevens in 1947. You can tour the lower fort area and Battery Russell, an emplacement that once housed two 10-inch shore guns. It was fired upon by a Japanese submarine during World War II.

Don't miss Fort Clatsop, the National Memorial at the site of Lewis and Clark's 1805-06 winter encampment.

Their fort has been reconstructed (photo, page 9), based upon Capt. William Clark's floor plan sketches. Wandering from room to room, you'll understand how those 33 history-making people must have lived. (Lewis and Clark led 27 soldiers; Toussaint Charbonneau and his wife, Sacajawea, and their infant son; and Clark's servant.) During summer, park rangers in buckskin garb demonstrate the loading and firing of flintlock rifles, the preparation of elk jerky, the rendering of fat, the making of lead rifle balls and candles, and the carving of dugout canoes.

The adjacent Visitor Center-Museum houses many impressive exhibits, including marvelous maps and verbal and pictorial excerpts from the explorers' journals. A 27-minute movie and a slide program describe the 7,689 — mile journey from St. Louis to the Pacific Ocean and back.

Fort Clatsop is open every day (except Christmas), from 8 a.m. - 7:30 p.m. in summer, and 8-5 in winter. It's about six miles southwest of Astoria. Cross the Young's Bay Bridge on Highway 101 west of Astoria, then turn south and follow the signs. There are picnic facilities. Admission: free.

Delightful side trips lead up river valleys and into the forest-clad hills of Clatsop County. I recommend the 30-mile Young's River Loop. Cross Young's Bay on Highway 101-Alt. south of the city (not Highway 101, west of town). A mile south of the bridge, a sign points left to the loop drive. You'll meander along the base of wooded hills, above the pretty tidewater stream and nearby dairy farms. Young's River Falls (photo, page 9) is a delightful spot for a picnic, a swim or a hike. Return to Astoria via Olney and Highway 202.

For further information about area tourist attractions, contact the Astoria Chamber of Commerce; it's at the Port of Astoria dock, P.O. Box 176, telephone 325-6311.

Above: Young's River Falls, a lovely spot near Astoria.

Fort Clatsop National Memorial marks the Lewis and Clark Expedition's 1805-06 winter encampment. You can tour the reconstructed fort, right, and the Visitor Center-Museum.

Looking across the Promenade and Turnaround to Seaside's popular beach and mighty Tillamook Head.

Seaside boasts the state's busiest and most popular beach.

It has been a leading coast resort since 1871, when railroad-shipping-stage coach magnate Ben Holladay built fabulous Seaside House near the cove just north of mighty Tillamook Head.

Seaside has dozens of motels, an expanded convention center, and thousands of vacation and

Seaside

weekend visitors. It also has the Oregon Coast's brightest lights. The Turnaround area, for example, lures tourists with an amusement park, assorted pinball and shooting galleries, an aquarium, bumper cars, various food stands, and related enterprises.

Most visitors approach Seaside from the north via Highway 101. But consider two alternatives. It's possible to drive down the beach at low tide, from Fort Stevens State Park 10 miles south to Gearhart. (Stay out of soft sand and wet spots, and observe the 25 mph speed limit.) Or there's a slow but pleasant drive up the Lewis and Clark River, from Fort Clatsop south to Seaside. The road intersects with Highway 101 just north of the Neawanna Creek bridge, at the north edge of Seaside.

Various points of interest can be reached from Highway 101 north of Seaside.

Golfers may be tempted by either of two fine courses. Astoria Country Club, eight miles north of Seaside, is private, with guest privileges. Gearhart Golf Links is a popular, 18-hole public course. There's another public course in the area, 9-hole Seaside Country Club.

Cullaby Lake County Park, seven miles north of Seaside, offers good swimming, boating, water skiing and fishing for crappies, bluegills, perch, catfish and large mouth bass. Its attractive picnic area has a community kitchen-shelter and playground equipment for the kids. Sunset Lake, just west of Cullaby, also has a park, picnic grounds, and good fishing for trout and most of the same species.

You'll find good beach access at Del Rey State Wayside and at Gearhart. The latter is a quiet but popular residential community along the beach north of Seaside. A large condominium complex has developed here in recent years, attracting numerous convention-goers as well as other tourists.

Seaside's Promenade gives it a distinction other beach resorts must envy. The massive concrete seawall and walkway extends along the oceanfront more than a mile and a half, from Avenue U north to 12th Avenue. It was constructed in 1921 to replace a storm-battered boardwalk and to protect oceanfront properties. You'll enjoy a stroll along the Prom, and the view of sand, surf and majestic Tillamook Head. Numerous benches provide places to rest for a minute or an hour, and stairways lead to the beach here and there. The Prom also is ideal for cycling from one end of town to the other.

The broad beach has deep, fine sand and a gentle slope down into the sea. Sun bathers and surf bathers flock here during the busy season. There's even playground equipment on the sand near the Turn-around, at the end of Broadway Street. It's one of Oregon's best razor clam beaches, especially on outgoing minus tides (except between July 15 and Aug. 31, when the season is closed between Tillamook Head and the Columbia River.) Surfers are drawn to the cove area south of town.

Fishermen enjoy the Necanicum River, which winds through town en route to the sea. It's a popular stream to catch cutthroat trout in late summer, salmon in the fall and steelhead in winter. Surf fishing is good along the beaches, and others drop lines off the rocks in the cove area.

If you're a hiker, don't even try to resist the scenic trail over 1,135-foot-high Tillamook Head to Ecola State Park. It's described on pages 12-13.

Another popular hike is the 1,700-foot climb up Saddle Mountain to its 3,283-foot summit (photo, page 11), the highest point in this corner of Oregon. From Seaside, drive south and east 14 miles on Highways 101 and 26, then north seven miles to Saddle Mountain State Park. It has a small campground, plus picnic and restroom facilities. More than 2,000 kinds of wildflowers have been identified in this park, which also abounds with deer. The trail climbs about three miles through woods and along rocky slopes to the summit. It's a safe trip for grade school-age youngsters. No special equipment is needed, although boots are helpful. You'll zigzag up a series of switchbacks to the saddle and then ascend a steep slope to the summit. It yields a magnificent view in all directions. You'll gaze west to the ocean, and north to Astoria and the mouth of the Columbia River. Far to the east, on a clear day, you'll see those great snowcapped peaks of the Cascades, mountains named Hood, Rainier, St. Helens, Adams and Jefferson.

Seaside has been designated the official end of the Lewis and Clark Trail. While spending the winter of 1805-06 at Fort Clatsop, the famous explorers estab-

Digging razor clams along the beach at low tide provides family fun and great eating. Razors are abundant on Clatsop County beaches.

lished a salt recovery station above the beach at present Seaside. They boiled an estimated 1,300 to 1,400 gallons of seawater over a period of seven weeks to get four bushels of salt, which they needed to preserve meats and other food for the long return trip. Their salt cairn has been reproduced from specifications in the Lewis and Clark diaries. It's on Lewis and Clark Way, eight blocks south of Broadway, between Beach Drive and the Promenade.

A number of special events are staged annually in Seaside. These include the Miss Oregon Pageant in July, a 26-mile Marathon race the last Saturday of February, and an 8-mile beach run and the Arts and Crafts Show each August.

For further information, contact the Seaside Chamber of Commerce, P.O. Box 7, telephone 738-6391.

The whole family can climb Saddle Mountain, the highest peak in Oregon's northwest corner.

At Ecola Point, there's a magnificent view south toward Haystack Rock and Cannon Beach.

Ecola State Park

Capt. William Clark, in 1806, described the view south from Tillamook Head as "the grandest and most pleasing prospects which my eyes every surveyed."

This remains a spectacularly beautiful shoreline today, perhaps the most scenic on the entire Oregon Coast.

Ecola State Park begins at the southern edge of Seaside. It extends south along seven miles of oceanfront past Tillamook Head, Indian Point and Ecola Point to Cannon Beach. The park itself covers more than 1,300 acres, and a recent bequest and land exchange resulted in creation of 605-acre Elmer Feldenheimer Forest Preserve just east of the park.

Most of the park's nearly 200,000 annual visitors drive to Cannon Beach and then four miles north to Ecola Point. It yields one of Oregon's most magnificent views (photo above), south over Crescent Beach and Chapman Point, past Haystack Rock, Arch Cape and Cape Falcon to mighty Neahkahnie Mountain. The surf pounds against the headland 75 feet below. Perhaps you'll observe sea lions sunning themselves

on offshore Arch Rock. Tillamook Rock and Lighthouse (photo, page 13) rise from the sea to the northwest. Delightful trails parallel the edge of Ecola Point and also descend to sandy Crescent Beach. You can survey the impressive seascape from some of the picnic tables, while others are in secluded spots under the trees.

Drive north two more miles to Indian Beach. A stretch of white sand nearly a mile long (photo, page 13), it's one of Oregon's most popular surfing beaches. Indians chose this lovely spot in centuries past, leaving mounds rich with artifacts. If you'd enjoy another beautiful view down the coast, walk across the bridge and up the trail toward Seaside a few hundred feet. Or take a short hike up Indian Creek to a pretty waterfall.

The best way to fully appreciate this marvelous coastline is to hike the Oregon Coast Trail. From Seaside, it's a six-mile trek over Tillamook Head to Indian Beach, or a 12-mile journey all the way to Cannon Beach. Drive (via Avenue U or Beach Street) out Edgewood Street south of Seaside to the parking lot at the end of the road. The trail takes a moderately steep climb the first two miles, up the north side of the head, through towering spruce and fir. Viewpoints provide a sweeping vista north, past Seaside and Gearhart. Then the trail turns south, through a mixture of virgin rain forest and cutover slopes. You'll look down sheer cliffs nearly 1,000 feet into the sea at various places. After about three delightful hours, you'll arrive at Indian Beach. If you haven't another car waiting in the parking lot, you can hike back to Seaside. Or you can walk six more miles to Cannon Beach, and catch a bus back to Seaside.

Tillamook Rock and its abandoned Lighthouse are visible from many places in the park. Rising 88 feet from the sea with nearly perpendicular sides, the government chose this tiny island as a lighthouse site in 1880. It proved extremely difficult to move people and supplies to and from the rock, via steel cables suspended between anchored ships and the lighthouse. Storms wreaked havoc over the years. Seawater regularly splashed across the rock and lighthouse. At times the raging sea hurled rocks through windows, walls and even the lighthouse lens. The government finally surrendered to the Pacific in 1957, abandoning the lighthouse and placing the rugged rock on the auction block. The 58 bids ranged from $2 up to $5,600, submitted by a combine of about 50 Las Vegas investors. Ownership changed hands again in 1973, 1978 and 1980, when an Oregon partnership paid $50,000 for the rock and lighthouse. The partners recently opened Eternity at Sea Columbarium, using the lighthouse as a depository for cremated human remains.

This seaside region has been plagued by a landslide problem for hundreds and perhaps thousands of years. The worst recent slide, in 1961, devastated the developed area at Ecola Point. One observer noted a slippage area more than 2,000 feet long and 360 feet wide, with soil 30 feet deep slipping toward the sea at a rate of six feet per day. The park was closed 18 months for repairs.

Ecola State Park dates back to 1932, when four generous Oregonians (named on the park's memorial marker) donated half of a 451-acre tract at Ecola Point, plus their oceanfront homes. The state purchased the other half from another owner for $17,500. One of the three state highway commissioners objected strenuously to such frivolous spending in the depth of the Depression. Fortunately, he didn't prevail.

Many Oregonians regard Ecola as the most beautiful of our state parks. Look it over carefully before casting your vote.

Upper right: Picnic tables in a serene setting at Ecola Point, with Tillamook Rock and Lighthouse in the background.

Indian Beach, a pleasant spot north of Ecola Point.

Framed by a gnarled tree, picturesque Haystack Rock dominates the oceanfront at Cannon Beach.

Cannon Beach to Arch Cape

Picturesque Cannon Beach is a delightful oceanfront town you shouldn't miss, one with a special challenge for every photographer.

Haystack Rock and two smaller sea stacks rise from the ocean floor, providing a majestic backdrop for the broad beach and shoreline. Numerous old trees stand just above the beach, with extended limbs gnarled by decades of wind off the sea just waiting to frame your picture.

If you carry a camera, you'll be struck by an irresistible urge to find the best way to bring all this beauty together in a single photograph.

Cannon Beach has developed into an art colony in recent years. Dozens of new shops include art galleries, antique, craft and gift shops. Many of the new and remodeled structures exhibit very tasteful architecture, and there's obvious pride in property maintenance.

Portland State University's "Haystack" workshops in music, writing and the visual arts attract hundreds of visitors for several weeks each summer. The P.S.U. Players stage excellent summertime dramatic productions. A concert series is held here each fall and winter, and local people produce the Dickens Festival each December.

Turn off Highway 101 at the northern Cannon Beach exit, about three miles south of the Highway 26 junction. It's about one-third mile down the hill to the turnoff to Ecola State Park (see pages 12-13). In another one-third mile, you'll reach beautiful downtown Cannon Beach.

Follow the Beach Loop for nearly three miles through Cannon Beach and adjoining Tolovana Park. You'll want to visit the beach at one or more of several good access points. Photographers should turn west to Ocean Avenue, which offers a beautiful perspective just above the beach. Don't miss the new Tolovana Beach Wayside, with parking, picnic and restroom facilities, nearly two miles south of the downtown area.

The beach scene here always focuses upon Haystack Rock, perhaps America's most photographed offshore monolith. (Note: There's another rock of the same name near Cape Kiwanda in Tillamook County, a source of continuing confusion.) Two rock pinnacles called The Needles stand just south of 235-foot-high Haystack. They have survived the pounding of the sea for thousands of years, but two similar sea stacks collapsed from the same onslaught early in this century. If you visit at low tide, you'll see starfish, sea anemones, hermit crabs and small fish in the rich tidal pools around Haystack. You may want to climb part way up the rock; it's now illegal to ascend beyond the point marked by signs.

The name "Cannon Beach" applies both to the city and to the beach that extends seven miles from Chapman Point south to Arch Cape. It's one of the prettiest and most appealing beaches along Oregon's entire coastline.

You can enjoy the beach from stopping places along Highway 101 south of Cannon Beach. Two fine new viewpoints have been constructed, for example, about a half-mile south of the Beach Loop's southern junction with the highway. There's a nice state wayside a mile south of the viewpoints, with trails leading down to the beach. And don't miss Hug Point State Park (photo, page 16), another mile south of the wayside.

In the early days, when wagons and later automobiles used the beach as a highway, it wasn't possible to get around Hug Point except at low tide. So the county built a road from the beach up to high ground here. You can see the remains of the old wagon road cut into the rock. There's a secluded beach, protected by the point from northerly winds. Picnic facilities don't include running water.

Downtown Cannon Beach features appealing specialty shops and attractive architecture.

Above: The view north toward Cannon Beach. Below: Feeding sea gulls near Haystack Rock.

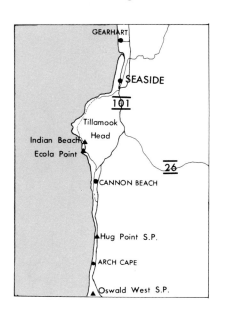

15

Above: Wading in the surf near Hug Point State Park, a delightful beach area. Right: The view south toward Arch Cape. Below: Hug Point protects a beachgoer from the northerly wind.

I strongly recommend a walk along all or part of the six-mile-long beach from Cannon Beach to Arch Cape. Time your trip for low tide, since it's dangerous or impossible to get around Silver Point, Humbug Point and Hug Point at high tide. Observe the other beach safety rules, too; avoid swimming on outgoing tides and beware of logs along the beach that can be moved or turned suddenly by large waves. Low tide best exposes the beautiful and distinctive rock formations along this beach and reveals remarkable marine life in the tidal pools. But don't remove or disturb the intertidal creatures; they are protected by law.

If you aren't equal to a six-mile hike down this beach, then explore part of it. Start at Hug Point and walk either to the north or south.

More vigorous hikers shouldn't overlook the scenic trail over Tillamook Head, described on pages 12-13. And if you want a more arduous all-day adventure, you can climb 2,775-foot Angora Peak. Drive south past most of the quiet seaside village of Arch Cape. About a quarter-mile north of the tunnel, veer left on Arch Cape Mill Road. Drive less than a half-mile and

park outside a gate that extends across the road. Walk through the gate and then turn right up the old logging road. It will lead you about four miles, nearly to the peak. There's a splendid view from the summit, up and down the coastline and east to the Cascade Mountains.

Capt. William Clark and several other members of the Lewis and Clark Expedition were the first whites to visit this area in 1806. They came from their winter quarters at Fort Clatsop and their salt cairn at Seaside to buy from the Indians blubber from a whale that had washed up on the beach. Clark named the area and a creek Ecola, the Clatsop word for whale. But early settlers renamed the stream Elk Creek. The village that grew south of the creek was named Elk Creek, then changed to Ecola, and finally to Cannon Beach. The latter name derived from a weapon that washed up on shore here. The cannon came from the schooner "Shark," which fell victim in 1846 to swift currents and shifting sandbars at the mouth of the Columbia River. The original gun is displayed at a roadside historical marker near Arch Cape; a replica stands beside another such sign east of Cannon Beach.

The beach here yields fine razor clams on outgoing minus tides. The fishing is limited, mostly from the

beaches or the rocks, although some cutthroat are caught in Elk and Arch Cape Creeks.

The annual Cannon Beach Sand Castle Contest is one of the Oregon Coast's finest special events. It's held on a Saturday morning each summer, after a high tide during the night dampens the sand. Several hundred builders of all ages and levels of artistry gather at dawn and mold imaginative creations in the wet sand. Unfortunately, however, the next high tide doesn't respect their handiwork.

For more information, contact the Cannon Beach Chamber of Commerce, P.O. Box 64, telephone 436-2623.

You'll circle mighty Neahkahnie Mountain on a dramatic highway, 700 feet above the pounding surf.

Oswald West State Park

More than five miles of particularly rugged and scenic coastline dominate remarkable Oswald West State Park.

Three bold headlands project into the blue Pacific — 900-foot-high Arch Cape at the northern end; beautiful Cape Falcon in the middle; and, to the south, 1,710-foot-high Neahkahnie Mountain, third highest peak on the entire Oregon Coast. Sheer cliffs drop hundreds of feet into the sea. Delightful Short Sand Beach nestles in Smuggler's Cove, between the protective shoulders of Neahkahnie Mountain and Cape Falcon. And the park is covered with a magnificent coastal rain forest of spruce and hemlock.

Appropriately, the park is named for the governor instrumental in preserving Oregon's beaches for public use.

You'll enter this four-square-mile park at Arch Cape tunnel. It's possible to drive straight through in a few minutes. But don't.

Stop at the main parking lot, 3½ miles south of the tunnel. A posted map shows the routes of some of Oregon's finest hiking trails.

Start with the easy half-mile trail down Short Sand Creek to the beach. You'll pass an appealing walk-in campground with 35 sites (wheelbarrows are provided to haul your camping gear.) The pleasant picnic area above the beach has tables, gas stoves, restrooms and water, plus a marvelous view across the sand and surf to Cape Falcon. This is Smuggler's Cove, reputedly a haven for pirates of yore, and indisputably a treasure for today's visitors.

After enjoying Short Sand Beach for five minutes or five hours, it's possible to return along the same creekside trail to the parking lot. But I recommend that you turn north on the trail just above the beach. You'll soon pass a memorial to Associated Press newsman Matt Kramer. His perceptive reporting of legislative handling of the 1967 beach bill inspired widespread public demand to guarantee public access to dry sand areas. Just north of the Kramer memorial, a trail turns east toward the highway. But I recommend proceeding 1.3 miles north and west to Cape Falcon. You'll walk through lush rain forest most of the way, emerging into sunshine on the cape. The beautiful view back toward the beach and Neahkahnie Mountain (photo, page 18) keeps getting more spectac-

Delightful Short Sand Beach nestles between Cape Falcon (hidden in the fog, at left) and Neahkahnie Mountain, below. It's an easy half-mile walk from the highway to the beach.

ular as you proceed out to the point. You'll appreciate the marvelous solitude, with stillness broken only by the rhythmic sound of the surf pounding against the cliffs below.

Most visitors return from the cape to the highway, completing a loop hike of about four miles, one of Oregon's best. But it's also possible to hike north from the cape, along rugged bluffs far above the sea (photo, page 19). The trail nears Highway 101 in about four miles, at a point about two miles north of the parking lot.

Or perhaps you feel frisky enough to conquer 1,710-foot-high Neahkahnie Mountain. A three-mile trail zigzags up its northern slope. You can begin near the picnic area at Short Sand Beach, or where the trail crosses the highway, just north of the viewpoint honoring Governor West, marked by a small sign east of the highway. It's a fairly arduous climb, but you'll be rewarded by a magnificent view from the summit, north beyond the Columbia River and south down the coast past Nehalem Bay to Cape Lookout (photo, page 20). You can return by the same route, or descend the

eastern and southern slopes on a one-mile route that returns to the highway just north of Neah-Kah-Nie Golf Course.

Whether or not you hike to its summit, you'll understand the spiritual reverence the native Indians felt for Neahkahnie Mountain. The highway grade has been chiseled or blasted into solid rock on the mountain's western and southern slopes, about 700 feet above the Pacific. Stop at one or more of the roadside viewpoints. Gaze down those sheer cliffs and out to sea. Then turn south, looking past Manzanita and Nehalem Bay to faraway Capes Meares and Lookout.

An old story about buried treasure on Neahkahnie Mountain continues to grip the imagination of many Oregonians. Sometime back in the 18th Century, Indians supposedly saw a ship anchor here and white sailors bury a chest on the mountain's southern slope. After digging a deep hole, the seamen supposedly murdered a Negro crewman and placed his body across the chest before covering it. There's just enough evidence to keep the story alive and to whet the appetites of numerous hole-digging treasure seekers. But so far all of Neahkahnie's recovered treasures have been scenic and spiritual.

At one of the mountain's roadside viewpoints, note the memorial to the foresighted statesman for whom this park is named.

Gov. Oswald West served from 1911-15. He's best remembered for what has been called saving Oregon's beaches for the public. He persuaded the 1913 Oregon Legislature to declare all state beaches a public highway and prohibit further sale of land between the low-tide and high-tide lines. (Note: From 1874 until 1913, the state had offered sale of tideland to owners of adjacent property, disposing of about 23 miles of oceanfront in 37 transactions. The beaches of Clatsop County previously had been declared a highway. So the act recommended and signed by Gov. West stopped the sale of state tideland south to the California line. More recently, legislators of 1967 and 1969 clarified state control of and public access to the so-called dry sands area, above the ordinary high-tide line and up to the vegetation line.)

West exercised remarkable vision in this and other respects. President Theodore Roosevelt once described him as "a man more intelligently alive to the beauty of nature . . . and more keenly appreciative of how much this natural beauty should mean to civilized mankind, than almost any other man I have ever met holding high political position. . . ."

We can be thankful that Gov. Oswald West staked the public's claim to Oregon's incomparable beaches back in 1913. It's hard to imagine a more appropriate name for this exceptional state park.

Above: Marvelous hiking trails penetrate the park's virgin rain forest. Right: North of Cape Falcon, the rugged coastline north to Arch Cape.

From the summit of Neahkahnie Mountain, hikers capture a marvelous view south past Nehalem Bay.

Neahkahnie to Tillamook Bay

Twin Rocks and the handsome arch, viewed from Rockaway's beach, through a telephoto lens.

Mighty coastal headlands and virgin rain forests dominate the land just north of Neahkahnie Mountain.

From its south slope, however, you'll view two of Oregon's major bays, a string of beach towns and picturesque fishing villages, lush coastal lowlands and tidewater streams.

Drive down the mountain, about a mile past scenic Neah-Kah-Nie Golf Course. Then turn west on Nehalem Road to Neahkahnie Beach (photo, page 21), with its pretty and protected setting just south of the great mountain. Drive south on Ocean Road, just above the beach, to Manzanita.

Now you may want to drive up the hillside to Highway 101. Or you can continue south above the beach on Carmel and Necarney Streets to a nearby state park and sand spit. This also is a good place for hikers to pick up the Oregon Coast Trail, which proceeds south down the beach about six miles to the mouth of Nehalem Bay. (Make advance arrangements for ferry service across the river, as explained in the coast trail brochure; it's available at most state parks or from the state parks office in Salem.)

Nehalem Bay State Park, a mile south of Manzanita, extends four miles down the spit that separates the ocean and bay. Its campground, open from mid-April through October, has 292 improved sites. Picnic facilities are located near the bayside boat ramp. There's another picnic area (without water) four miles down the beach at the end of the spit, accessible by foot or boat.

Highway 101 circles the bay, through the communities of Nehalem, Wheeler and Brighton. Nehalem, which hosts the Nehalem Arts and Crafts Festival each July, has a number of attractive shops for antiques and craft items. Boat ramps and marinas serve fishermen at several spots along the bay and river, including a public ramp south of Nehalem and another at Wheeler. The bay is noted for excellent year-round crabbing, for soft-shell clams on the tide flats opposite Wheeler, and for salmon, flounder and perch. The Nehalem River is a good producer of salmon and steelhead.

South of Nehalem, consider a one-mile side trip on Highway 53 to the sleepy village of Mohler. A former cheese factory there has been converted into the Nehalem Bay Winery, where you can sample fruit wines most afternoons. (It's part of a "Food, Cheese and Wine Tour," which also includes stops at the Tillamook cheese factory, at sausage and oyster houses at Bay City, and at the Garibaldi wharf.) From Mohler, there's a pretty drive east up the Nehalem River, past Roy Creek County Park about seven miles to Nehalem Falls and a state forestry campground. Or there's another scenic drive to the south, up Foley

Creek and then down the Miami River to Garibaldi and Highway 101.

After rounding Nehalem Bay, the highway parallels the broad, sandy beach for more than five miles south to Tillamook Bay. You'll pass Nedonna Beach, Manhattan Beach, Rockaway and Twin Rocks. Numerous tourist facilities are available, especially at Rockaway, where a state wayside provides fine beach access. Lake Lytle is a popular place for swimming, sailing, waterskiing and fishing for trout and bass. Twin Rocks is named for two offshore sea stacks (photo, page 20), one of which has a handsome arch. It's a remnant of an ancient cave which the pounding surf carved into those rocks when they were part of an earlier shoreline.

Barview County Park attracts fishermen, who catch perch, flounder and bottom fish off the jetty at the mouth of Tillamook Bay. It has 164 campsites, picnic facilities and nearby sand dunes.

Garibaldi, about two miles from the mouth of Tillamook Bay, is the area's prime fishing mecca. It's Oregon's fifth busiest commercial fishing port, ranking behind only Astoria, Coos Bay, Newport and Winchester Bay. Several charter firms operate here, specializing in ocean forays for salmon. Sportsmen also catch salmon, cutthroat and steelhead that are passing through the bay en route to spawning beds in tributary streams. The picturesque wharf area (photo, page 21) includes a boat basin, several seafood plants and restaurants. You can observe shrimp processing at Smith Pacific Shrimp between April and mid-October. In addition to the shrimp, the bay also yields abundant crab and clams, and more than two-thirds of the state's commercial oyster crop.

The Miami River, just beyond Garibaldi, provides good cutthroat and rainbow trout fishing. But for salmon and steelhead, it isn't the equal of more noted

Above: Neahkahnie Beach and Mountain.

Below: Fishing boats in Tillamook Bay.

Tillamook Bay tributaries further south — the Trask, Wilson, Tillamook and Kilchis Rivers.

Bay City, six miles north of Tillamook, has a city park where you can picnic or camp along a creek under the trees, near tennis courts and playground equipment.

For further information about tourist attractions throughout Tillamook County, contact the Chamber of Commerce, 2105 First Street, Tillamook 97141, telephone 842-7525.

Fishing boats moored at Garibaldi boat basin.

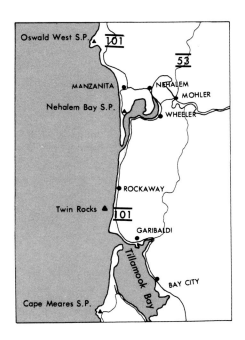

Cape Meares Loop

View across Short Beach, looking north to Cape Meares.

You can take a loop trip of only about 20 miles from Tillamook past Cape Meares, Oceanside and Netarts.

But rather than return to the county seat, I strongly recommend continuing south past Capes Lookout and Kiwanda. Three Capes Scenic Drive is a never-to-be-forgotten journey of about 40 miles (not counting a 25-mile return to Tillamook.) See the map on page 23.

You'll follow the shore of Tillamook Bay between Tillamook and Cape Meares. A county boat launch provides access to the bay for varied fishing and excellent year-round crabbing (see page 21.) Clams are abundant in the tide flats near the Lake Meares dike, but stay out of the commercial shrimp and oyster beds. The lake is stocked with rainbow trout.

Back in 1907, real estate men promoted a fabulous new resort on Bayocean Peninsula, the sand spit north of Cape Meares between the ocean and Tillamook Bay. They platted a city and sold more than 2,000 lots, before going bankrupt during World War I. But Pacific Ocean storms clobbered the vulnerable spit every few

Oceanside clings to the hillside above the beach.

years, causing increasing erosion and gradual abandonment of Bayocean property. A great storm completely breached the spit in 1953. You can drive about a mile onto the spit via South Jetty Road, which crosses the Lake Meares dike. A hike of less than a mile will take you to the site of old Bayocean, but there's only scant evidence of the former resort. It's another three miles to the end of the spit.

Cape Meares State Park offers much worth seeing. Stroll down the paved path from the parking lot to the lighthouse. You'll see and hear the surf thundering against steep sea cliffs 200 feet below. Congress authorized construction of this lighthouse on Cape Lookout, 10 miles to the south. But the builders and their ox teams confused one remote seacoast headland for another in 1890, and constructed it on the cape named for British navigator John Meares. It was deactivated in 1963, and is usually open to the public on summer weekends.

Take the short trail from the parking lot past the restrooms and picnic area to the Octopus Tree (photo, page 23.) This giant Sitka spruce has a circumference of nearly 50 feet. Six huge limbs branch out along the ground and then turn upward, resembling an enormous candelabra. A trail continues from the tree area along the south side of the cape, providing a beautiful view past Short Beach to Cape Lookout (photo, page 23.) There's another trail from the park entrance 1.2 miles along the north side of the cape. So it's possible to hike around a loop of less than three miles, including a connecting link along the highway. See the trail map sign near the park entrance.

Some of the Oregon Coast's most spectacular rock formations are located between Cape Meares and Oceanside, just south of Short Beach. There's a steep

Right: There's a lovely view from Cape Meares, south down the beach to Cape Lookout.

Below: At Cape Meares State Park, don't miss the Octopus Tree, a gigantic Sitka spruce.

and difficult path down to the beach near the mouth of Short Creek, 1.3 miles south of the park entrance.

Oceanside is a pretty village that clings to the hillside about two miles south of Cape Meares (photo, page 22.) It has a delightful beach, and just offshore you'll see scenic Three Arch Rocks, a federal refuge for thousands of sea birds and numerous sea lions. At the north end of the beach, the 120-foot-long tunnel through rugged Maxwell Point has been closed. But it's possible, at low tide, to hike around the point to a secluded cove and Agate Beach.

The highway continues south from Oceanside to Netarts, winding along hillsides far above the Pacific. A county launch at Netarts provides boat access to shallow, five-mile-long Netarts Bay. It's one of the state's most popular clamming areas, especially in the mud flats along the north edge of the bay and in midbay tidelands at times of minus tides. Dungeness crabs are caught in rings lowered from boats. The fishing isn't great, but perch and flounder are taken.

It's about seven miles from Netarts back to Tillamook. But I recommend that you continue south on Three Capes Scenic Drive.

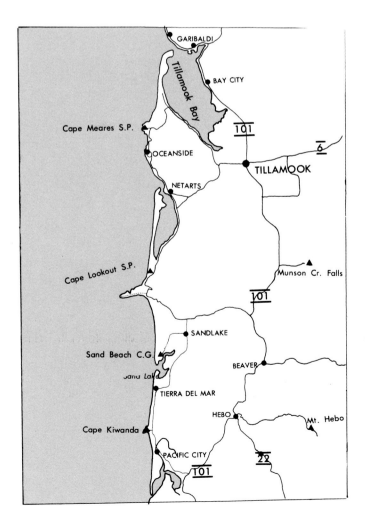

You'll get marvelous views along the Tillamook County coast from the shoulders of Cape Lookout – south past Sand Lake, Cape Kiwanda and the southerly Haystack Rock to Cascade Head, above; and north past Netarts Bay to Cape Meares, below.

Cape Lookout

Cape Lookout is perhaps the most rugged, dramatic and scenic headland on the entire Pacific Coast.

Its steep backbone of tough volcanic rock juts nearly two miles into the sea. There, for 20 million years, it has endured a pounding surf that chewed away flabbier material on its flanks.

One of Oregon's finest state parks is dominated by the mighty cape. The park also extends more than five miles up the beach north of the cape and includes the sand spit that separates Netarts Bay from the ocean. A lovely coastal rain forest of spruce, hemlock and red cedar grows above the beaches and sea cliffs. It's a sanctuary for more than 150 identified species of birds, including thousands of murres which nest on rocky ledges at the western end of the cape.

Located 12 miles southwest of Tillamook, you'll approach the cape from the north by a road that follows the shore of Netarts Bay. It's one of Oregon's most popular bays for clamming and crabbing (see page 23).

Thousands of visitors use the picnic area and campground which have been developed north of the cape. More than 50 picnic tables are scattered above the beach (photo, page 25), near sheltered electric stoves, bathhouse and restrooms. The campground has sites for 193 tents and full utility hookups for 53 trailers; for reservations from mid-May to Labor Day, mail your request and a $4 advance deposit to the park, at 13000 Whiskey Creek Rd., Tillamook, Ore. 97141. Two nearby self-guided nature trails give insight to the park's remarkable flora and fauna.

The highway continues south over the 800-foot-high ridge that extends east from the cape. From Anderson Viewpoint, on the north slope, you look north across Netarts Bay and sand spit to Cape Meares. Just across the summit, there's a marvelous vista south past Sand Lake, picturesque Cape Kiwanda and Haystack Rock to mighty Cascade Head.

If you're a hiker, don't miss the exciting 2½-mile trail from the parking lot near the summit out to the point. It's a fairly easy walk near the ridge of the cape, with frequent views south along the coast and down those sheer basaltic cliffs more than 500 feet into the sea. The trail passes the place (marked by a plaque) where a B-17 bomber crashed in 1943. You'll hear the haunting sounds of a warning buoy a half-mile northwest of the cape before you see it.

Few Oregon trails can match this one for either scenery or solitude. But muddy spots make boots advisable, and steep dropoffs require caution concerning young children. If a round trip of five miles and more than two hours intimidates you, a 10-15 minute walk will take you under towering trees to the first great viewpoint.

Cape Lookout is worthwhile for those who explore by automobile, but it reserves its greatest treats for hikers.

Above: Cape Lookout State Park has a nice beach.

Below: View down the north side of the cape.

Cape Kiwanda

Fishermen launch a dory across the beach near lovely Cape Kiwanda.

The Oregon Coast has many headlands that rise higher or project farther into the sea. But none are more picturesque than Cape Kiwanda, or more challenging for a photographer.

The cape is a ridge of yellowing sandstone, with majestic sedimentary contours and concave indentations that have been carved out by the pounding surf. To its front, a quarter-mile at sea, stands 327-foot-high Haystack Rock. Huge sand dunes rise to its rear, and perfect sand beaches stretch far to its north and south.

It's lovely in bright sunshine, or at sunset, as photographs on these pages testify. And it's something to behold in winter storms, when the ocean's fury whips waves 75 feet or more into the air. They sometimes come crashing over its saddle and down the cape like a mountain waterfall.

Cape Kiwanda's special romance is enhanced by the hundreds of fishermen who regularly take their dories to sea across the beach just south of the cape. This is one of the few places on the entire Pacific Coast where it's possible to launch small vessels directly off the beach and into the breakers.

You probably will approach the cape from the north, either from Cape Lookout via Three Capes Scenic Drive or from a connecting road to Highway 101 and Tillamook. If so, you will drive past Sand Lake, several miles north of the cape. It really isn't a lake, but rather a very shallow bay or tidal basin off the ocean.

Northern Oregon's most popular dunes area for dunebuggies, sand-equipped motor bikes and sand fleas is just north of Sand Lake. Turn at Sandlake Grocery two miles west to Sand Beach (Forest Service) Campground, which has 101 campsites near the bay and ocean. The Northwest Trail and Dune Association sponsors races here six weekends each summer. Automobiles are modified for the dunes in various ways, equipped with fat, underinflated paddle tires. Time trials are held Saturday mornings, followed by the drag races Saturday afternoons and Sundays. Motorcycle races also are held north of the campground several weekends per year. For schedules, call Sandlake Grocery (965-6152) or Hebo Ranger Station (392-3161). On summer holiday weekends, the area is so popular that the Forest Service requires permits limited to 1,700 vehicles; phone or write the Hebo Ranger Station, Hebo, Ore.

Further south, Tillamook County's Whalen Island Park has 40 campsites and picnic facilities on a peninsula in Sand Lake. It's a good place to catch flounder, salmon, cutthroat and steelhead, as well as for clamming and crabbing. The shallow water is ideal for children's swimming.

The road continues south past sleepy Tierra Del Mar and down the beach, swinging inland just north of the cape.

Dorymen have been going to sea off the beach south of the cape for more than a half century. They use unique, flat-bottomed boats, descendants of the fishing dories of New England. They started crossing the beach at about the time commercial fishing was banned in the Nestucca River in the mid-1920's. Their number increased in the 1940's, when new outboard motors replaced oarpower. (Previously, some dorymen rowed all the way to Cape Lookout early in the morning and drifted back to Cape Kiwanda with the northerly wind in the afternoon.) But as recently as the 1950's, only about two dozen dories were launched regularly each day during the summer and early fall fishing season. Now hundreds of commercial and sports fishermen go to sea early each morning during the season, seeking salmon and sometimes tuna as far away as 50 miles. If the fishing is good, they won't return until late afternoon. The parade home is a daily ritual that usually attracts an audience. Each returning doryman catches a wave off the cape, guns his motor, and skids as far up on the beach as possible, toward his waiting boat trailer.

All the fishing isn't done at sea, however. The Nestucca River, which winds past Woods and Pacific City, within a mile of the cape, is one of Oregon's finest fishing rivers. It's second only to the Rogue River as a producer of fighting steelhead, and among the state's best half-dozen salmon streams. It's also known for cutthroat trout, and sportsmen find crabs and clams in the shallow bay.

The beach is broad, with gentle slopes and fine sand, extending north about four miles to Sand Lake and south the same distance along Nestucca Spit State Park to the mouth of the river. The beach south of the cape is a popular place for surf bathing and sun bathing, for picnics, and for watching the dories come and go. It's one of the state's best surfing beaches, thanks to the cape's protection, the fine sand, and a reef that extends from the cape to Haystack Rock and which creates great surfing waves. Occasionally, you'll even see sailboaters, in Hobie Cat catamarans.

And who can resist those huge dunes that rise behind the cape? It's a long, slow climb from the beach through deep sand for several hundred feet up the steep slope. But the return trip is a thriller. You may come racing pell-mell down the slope on your feet. But don't be surprised if you trip, fall, tumble or roll before you reach the bottom, breathlessly.

Walk out on the cape, assuming you're vigorous enough to climb up its shoulder through deep sand. The view from the top is gorgeous in all directions — north toward Cape Lookout (photo, page 27), south along the beach, and down those steep slopes into the sea. Fishermen drop their lines off the rocks. Sadly, a number of lives have been lost by people who went near the cape's edge, the reason for all those warning signs and safety fences.

Hang gliders use the north side of the cape most days in spring, summer and fall. It's exciting to watch them race part way down the slope, then catch a tailwind and soar into the air. Sometimes they ride an air current for hundreds of feet before alighting on the beach.

When you are ready to leave the Cape Kiwanda area, two major roads lead east from Pacific City to Highway 101. But you'll probably stay longer than you planned. For there's something magnetic about the lovely cape and all those dories.

Cape Kiwanda is photographed in many moods—including bright summer sunshine, above; shortly after sunset, below; and in raging winter storms.

Below: Sandstone sea cliffs north of Cape Kiwanda.

Tillamook to Oretown

Above: Munson Creek Falls, highest waterfall in the Coast Range. Below: Rain forest near the falls.

Tillamook isn't a beach town, but it's a crossroads for numerous nearby coastal attractions.

It's the northern terminus for Three Capes Scenic Drive, a marvelous loop past Capes Meares, Lookout and Kiwanda. (See pages 22-27.)

Fishermen go to sea from nearby Garibaldi or Pacific City. Other anglers prefer four major coastal bays — Tillamook, Netarts, Nehalem and Nestucca. The immediate Tillamook area also offers great stream fishing. Oregon has few finer salmon rivers than the Trask, which also produces plenty of steelhead and trout. The Wilson River is one of the state's premier steelhead streams. The Kilchis and the Tillamook also yield salmon, steelhead and cutthroat trout.

Most Tillamook visitors stop at its famous cheese factory, Oregon's largest producer of cheddar cheese. Abundant rain grows lush grass here, ideal dairy country. The remote location forced pioneer dairymen to convert their milk into cheese. Today, about 250 million pounds of milk is used to produce 25 million pounds of cheese annually. You can see the process through big observation windows, from 9-5 seven days per week. Wall exhibits, a public address system and brochures help explain the process. (There's a new and much smaller cheese factory just south of the big one; it produces rare French brie cheese.)

Another "must" is the Tillamook County Pioneer Museum at the north end of downtown, across from the county courthouse. Thousands of exhibits illustrate pioneer and Indian life in the county, including a replica of a pioneer home. Best of all, the second floor has an outstanding collection of more than 500 stuffed birds and mammals. The late Alex Walker created numerous dioramas portraying wildlife in representations of their natural habitat. The museum is open weekdays from 8:30 a.m. to 5 p.m., and Sundays from 1-5 p.m., but it's closed on Mondays from October through April. Admission: free.

Highway 101 proceeds south from Tillamook through lush inland valleys. If you must choose between the inland route and Three Capes Scenic Drive, take the latter. But if you have time for both, there's much of interest along Highway 101.

Three miles south of Tillamook, you'll see two huge hangars that were built by the U.S. Navy in 1942 to house coastal defense blimps. They are 1,100 feet long, 300 feet wide and 195 feet high, and have been converted into a sawmill and plywood plant. A nearby county park has picnic facilities and a hiking trail. There's another nice picnic spot at a state wayside about two miles further south above the Tillamook River.

About seven miles south of Tillamook, turn east 1½ miles to Munson Creek Falls County Park. The 319-foot falls is the highest in the Coast Range (photo, page 28.) It's surrounded by a coastal rain forest, where mighty spruce, hemlock and fir shield a lush understory of ferns and mosses. An easy walk on the lower trail along the gurgling creek takes you to a picnic table, in a setting of almost total solitude, and a good view of the falls. From the upper trail, it's possible to scramble down a steep bank to the base of the falls.

At Hemlock, four miles further south, a road goes west to Sandlake, Cape Lookout and Cape Kiwanda. Less than a half-mile beyond, another road goes east up the scenic East Fork of Beaver Creek.

At Beaver, the highway meets the Nestucca River. It will follow the pretty stream between wooded hills for about seven miles, until the river turns west near Cloverdale. The "Big Nestuc'" is one of Oregon's finest steelhead streams, and also attracts good runs of salmon and cutthroat trout. You can turn east up the river at Beaver, past Blaine and five public campgrounds on the upper reaches. Continuing south on the highway, there's a nice picnic spot along the river at Farmer's Creek.

Hebo, 19 miles south of Tillamook, is the terminus of Highway 22. It goes southeast along pretty Three Rivers, past a Forest Service campground toward Valley Junction and Salem. If you can spare an hour for a side trip, turn east on Highway 22 a quarter-mile and watch for the sign pointing left toward Mt. Hebo. A paved road winds up the mountain to the 3,174-foot summit, the highest point for many miles in all directions. A delightful Forest Service campground at pretty Hebo Lake has 10 campsites and picnic facilities (photo, at right.) The lake is stocked with trout. A large Air Force radar station (closed to the public) is located at the first of two summits, eight miles above Hebo, where there's a marvelous view north across the county and west to the sea. The Forest Service has two more campgrounds several miles east of the radar station.

About three miles south of Cloverdale, a road turns west past Woods to Pacific City. If you haven't taken Three Capes Scenic Drive, here's your last chance to see beautiful Capes Kiwanda, Lookout and Meares.

If you continue south, you'll soon cross the Little Nestucca River. It's a popular trout stream (photo, upper right.) There's an exceptionally pretty drive up the valley and canyon of the Little Nestucca. A county park three miles above Highway 101 offers a nice picnic spot under towering trees above the river.

Information about tourist attractions throughout Tillamook County may be obtained from the Chamber of Commerce, 2105 First Street, Tillamook 97141, telephone 842-7525.

Above: Fishermen line the banks of the Little Nestucca River. Below: Dairy cows graze near Hebo.

Below: Lovely Hebo Lake.

From Cascade Head, you look south past the Salmon River, Lincoln City, Devil's Lake and Siletz Bay.

Cascade Head and Neskowin

The Cascade Head-Neskowin area is the next major coastal attraction south of Cape Kiwanda and the Nestucca.

Cascade Head rises from the sea to an elevation of 1,770 feet. It's the loftiest point along the Oregon Coast, slightly higher than more dramatic Humbug Mountain (1,756 feet) and Neahkahnie Mountain (1,710 feet). The charming village of Neskowin nestles along the beach to its north, and the pretty Salmon River meanders along its southern flank.

Highway 101 winds over and around high hills south of Nestucca Bay. Delightful beaches to the west are mostly unseen and inaccessible, except via the Camp Winema road, a half-mile south of Oretown.

Neskowin, with its long expanse of white-sand beach, was a favorite resort even before construction of the coast highway in the 1920's. It's small, relatively quiet and family-oriented, despite the addition of a 190-room condominium complex in recent years. A state wayside provides parking, restrooms and beach access. Little Neskowin Creek winds across the beach,

creating wading spots for small children, before entering the Pacific at the foot of Proposal Rock. You may want to climb the latter at low tide; beware, it was named for couples stranded there at high tide, for better or for worse. Neskowin has two nine-hole golf courses, a riding stable, and an ideal atmosphere for quiet family vacationing.

Cascade Head looms to the south. It's part of the 15-square-mile Cascade Head Scenic-Research Area, created by Congress in 1974 and managed by Siuslaw National Forest. Its purpose is to protect the rugged headland, five miles of beautiful coastline, the delicate Salmon River estuary, and the area's abundant wildlife and flora.

Rain forest covers most of the headland, thanks to moderate marine temperatures, frequent fog, and nearly 100 inches of annual precipitation. Sitka spruce and hemlock shield a lush understory of mosses, ferns and varied shrubs. Most of the big trees rose from the ashes of a great fire that swept through here about 130 years ago, but some giant survivors of that blaze date back 250 years. Black-tailed deer roam through the woods, and experts have identified more than 370 species of wildlife (including 230 birds, 74 fish, 56 mammals) in the forest and rich river estuary.

Hikers shouldn't miss two splendid trails. Both are reached from Road 1861 (map, page 31), which turns west off Highway 101 at the summit, 3½ miles south of Neskowin.

A viewpoint 2.4 miles up that road yields a fine view south down the coast. Stay left on 1861 at 2.5 miles (unless you want to visit northern viewpoints.) At 3.2 miles, Road 1861 veers right and a Nature Conservancy trail starts down a Jeep path to the left. An easy 20-minute walk takes you through the woods and out on a grassy slope about 1,300 feet above the sea. The view south is magnificent (photo, page 30), past the Salmon River, Lincoln City, Devil's Lake and Siletz Bay to Cape Foulweather. You may want to continue down the long slope toward the sea, and then up a 529-foot-high knob called The Pinnacle. (Note: It's also

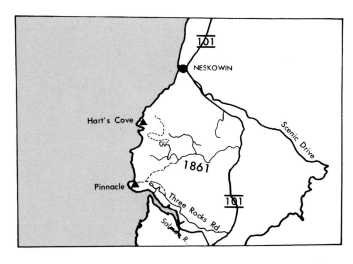

possible to follow another Nature Conservancy trail to this scenic point above the crashing sea. The other trail leaves Cascade Head Ranch, off Three Rocks Road. It climbs through spruce and alder woods and across the grassy headland nearly two miles to The Pinnacle.)

Another great hiking trail (No. 1303) penetrates about three miles of lush rain forest to lovely and tranquil Hart's Cove. Continue on Road 1861. At 3.5 miles, stay left at an unsigned junction. Proceed about three-fourths of a mile to the end of the road. The trail descends the canyons of Cliff and Chitwood Creeks on a zigzag northward course, above the shoreline and past a colony of barking sea lions. The trail emerges from deep woods into a secluded meadow, which· slopes down to cliffs at the edge of the sea just north of the scenic cove. You can hike to Hart's Cove and back in three hours. But plan to spend an additional hour or more in this serene and delightful spot, preferably over a picnic lunch.

Gulls, as well as people, enjoy Neskowin Creek as it winds across the sandy beach at Neskowin.

At the south foot of Cascade Head, turn west off Highway 101 on Three Rocks Road. It winds along the north bank of the Salmon River, a favorite area of Indians prior to white settlement in the 1870's. Indians lived well here, eating clams, shellfish and salmon they caught in the rich estuary, plus deer from the nearby forest. More than two miles west of the highway, the road forks south to a county boat ramp and north to Cascade Head Ranch, an attractive housing development on the hillsides above the sea. The ramp provides access to the river, one of Oregon's best small streams for salmon and steelhead fishing.

You'll enjoy the 10-mile Neskowin Scenic Drive, if time permits. Once part of the coast highway, it passes through the Cascade Head Experimental Forest, past the Neskowin Creek campground and picnic area. Experimental forestry practices are explained by signs at several turnoffs. The route leaves the highway a mile south of Neskowin and returns just north of the Salmon River.

For further information about the Cascade Head area, contact Siuslaw National Forest's Ranger Station at Hebo.

Wading in the surf at Neskowin, near Proposal Rock, with Cascade Head looming to the south.

20 Miracle Miles

Enjoy both the creek and the surf at Fogarty Creek State Park.

What's miraculous about the 20 Miracle Miles?

Nature has provided here a series of splendid beaches, scenic headlands, Siletz Bay, and Oregon's most picturesque harbor. Man has added the Oregon Coast's greatest concentration of motels (more than 1,600 rooms), plus numerous restaurants, art galleries, gift shops and other tourist-oriented businesses.

You'll return to the coast at Lincoln City. Just inside its north city limits, turn right to Roads End State Wayside. It provides access to a lovely beach known for agates and jasper. At low tide, you can hike around the point to the north, past rich tidal pools to a scenic cove.

Tourist-oriented businesses line the highway through Lincoln City. If you'd like to see more than 4,000 dolls in varied costumes, visit Lacey's Doll Museum, 3400 N. Highway 101.

Devil's Lake, a two-mile-long jewel east of Lincoln City, is surrounded by three nice parks, trees, and hundreds of homes. You can turn east at 14th Street for either a quick glimpse or the 10-mile loop around

Sailing on pretty Devil's Lake near Lincoln City.

the lake. Its shallow, relatively warm water attracts swimmers and waterskiers. You'll see sailboats most summer and fall afternoons (photo, page 32.) Many world speedboat records have been set at the major hydroplane races that are held here each Fourth of July and the last weekend of September. Fishermen catch trout, catfish and bass.

You can camp at Devil's Lake State Park, one block east of Highway 101 at N. 6th Drive. Open April to mid-October, the park has 68 tent and 32 trailer sites with full utility hookups; for reservations from mid-May to Labor Day, mail your request and $4 advance deposit to the park (1452 N.E. 6th, Lincoln City, 97367.) East Devil's Lake State Park, on the south shore, has picnic facilities and a boat ramp. A county park on the east shore has picnic tables and a roped-off swimming area.

D River State Wayside provides easy access to the wide, sandy beach which extends from Roads End south to Siletz Bay. D River, which flows 440 feet from Devil's Lake to the ocean, has been recognized by Guinness as the world's shortest river. There's a public boat landing nearby.

Highway 101 continues south, over the heights north of Siletz Bay. At the foot of the hill, turn west on S. 51st Street to the Taft dock and the mouth of the bay, a popular place for fishing and crabbing (photo, page 33.)

Consider three tempting side trips into the hills to the east. You can turn at S. 51st and follow Schooner Creek Road, either five miles upstream to a Forest Service campground or the long and scenic loop east and north to Rose Lodge. One mile further south, you can turn up Drift Creek Road. There's a 1914-model covered bridge 1½ miles east and a half-mile south, or continue 10 miles via Road 19 to a Forest Service camp and picnic area along pretty North Creek. A much longer side trip, beginning another mile south, follows Highway 229 up the twisting Siletz River to the village of Siletz. It was the headquarters of an Indian reservation that once covered most of the county.

The highway circles Siletz Bay, a popular place for fishing, crabbing and clamming. The Siletz River is one of Oregon's best streams for salmon, steelhead and cutthroat trout. Crabbers lower rings from boats or docks in the Taft and Kernville area. The mud flats between Kernville and Cutler City yield clams at low tide.

While circling the bay, note the handsome homes profiled on the sand spit to the west. They are part of Salishan, a premier resort and housing development which also has an outstanding 18-hole golf course. The ocean has menaced homes built on the sandspit, however. Winter storms in 1972-73 toppled one and seriously threatened several others.

You can picnic under fir and pines at Gleneden Beach State Wayside. Trails descend to the beach.

Fogarty Creek State Park (photo, page 32) is one of the state's most popular beaches. Bluffs north and south provide wind protection and ideal conditions for surf or sun bathing. It's fun to wade in the creek that meanders across the beach. Full picnic and bathhouse facilities are provided. Thousands attend the annual Depoe Bay Indian-Style Salmon Bake here on the first Saturday after Labor Day.

At Boiler Bay State Park, a mile south of Fogarty, you can stand on a rocky outcropping and watch big ocean waves crash against 40-foot-high sea cliffs. A ship burned at sea in 1910 and was beached in the nearby scenic inlet; its boiler still is visible at low tide. The park is a fine place to picnic or to fish from the rocks. A steep, unimproved trail descends from a nearby parking lot to the beach and tidal pools

Fishing off the beach at the mouth of Siletz Bay.

teeming with purple sea urchins, anemones, orange starfish, mussels and hermit crabs.

Picturesque Depoe Bay (photo, page 33) claims the world's smallest navigable harbor, six acres. Three charter firms take thousands of fishermen on four-hour forays for salmon or bottom fish. Short scenic cruises are offered, too. It's fun to watch the pilots steer their vessels through the narrow opening to the harbor, one cut through tough basalt the last 14 million years by tiny Depoe Creek. Various tourist-oriented businesses include an aquarium.

Rocky Creek State Park is adjacent to pretty Whale Cove, about two miles south of Depoe Bay. The park offers good fishing off the rocks and scenic picnic spots where you can watch the surf pound against basalt cliffs. A trail north of the park drops to the south side of the secluded cove, named for an 80-foot-long whale that washed up here in 1903.

For more information, contact the 20 Miracle Miles Chamber of Commerce, 3939 N.W. Highway 101, P.O. Box 797, Lincoln City, telephone 994-3070.

A fishing boat returns to Depoe Bay's tiny harbor.

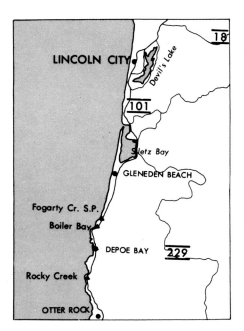

Cape Foulweather

Stop at Otter Crest Wayside on a lovely summer day and absorb that gorgeous view to the south, past Yaquina Head.

If you wonder how such a pleasant place was named Cape Foulweather, return during a winter storm. Capt. James Cook, the famed British navigator, discovered and named this headland during a raging storm in 1778.

The cape is another of Oregon's bold coastal headlands, the largest between Cascade Head and Cape Perpetua. It's a relatively young one, resulting from an underground lava flow about 15 million years ago.

Otter Crest Wayside is a magnificent viewpoint. Located at the cape's 453-foot-high summit, it's just off Highway 101 about eight miles north of Newport. Views both south and north are illustrated on these pages. You'll hear mighty waves crashing against the sea cliffs below. Fishing boats usually can be seen offshore, dancing on the sea caps. Sea lions and sea birds rest and nest on nearby islands, the high points of an ancient lava flow that now forms an offshore reef.

Drive around the cape on scenic Otter Crest Loop as well as over it via Highway 101. The former winds around rocky points, past one of the coast's great resorts and beautiful shoreline scenery en route to Otter Rock, on the cape's south flank.

Devil's Punchbowl State Park, at Otter Rock, features the remnant of an old sea cave. The surf carved two tunnel-like entrances through the yellowing sandstone. Then the roof collapsed, revealing the "punchbowl" depicted at the right. It's more dramatic at high tide, especially during a storm, when waves from two directions collide in the center. The resulting swirling mass of froth and foam may remind you of the interior of a washing machine, as well as a witch's cauldron.

The park has complete picnic facilities, restrooms, and a paved trail above the sea, from which you'll enjoy marvelous views. Marine Gardens, a few hundred feet to the north, reveals a wonderland of tidal pools at low tide. You'll see abundant starfish, purple sea urchins, mussels and other intertidal creatures here. State and federal laws prevent removing or disturbing them.

Left: Otter Crest yields a beautiful view south,

past Otter Rock and Beverly Beach to Yaquina Head.

Above: The view north from Otter Crest.

Below: A calm moment in Devil's Punch Bowl.

Both fishing and sightseeing draw visitors to picturesque Yaquina Bay at Newport.

Newport is Oregon's third-ranking sports and commercial fishing port, as well as the central coast's largest city and a major tourist center.

After stopping at Otter Crest and Otter Rock (pages 34-35), you'll drive down the coast past Beverly Beach State Park. It has picnic facilities and a beautiful beach, backed by sandstone sea cliffs in which 20-million-year-old fossils have been found. The park's year-round campground has sites for 152 tents and 127 trailers; for reservations from mid-May to Labor Day, mail your request and $4 advance deposit to the park (Star Route North, Box 684, Newport 97365.)

Newport

Continue south past Moolack Beach to Yaquina Head, an eroded seafront volcano of relatively recent vintage. Turn west at 52nd Street for a scenic drive out Lighthouse Road. Yaquina Head Lighthouse (photo, page 37) was constructed in 1873, to replace the unsatisfactory Yaquina Bay beacon.

Agate Beach is the lovely seafront south of Yaquina Head. It's a favorite of beachcombers and surfers. Agate Beach Wayside, in north Newport, offers beach access, parking, and picnic and restroom facilities.

Thousands of fishermen cross the Yaquina Bay bar

Seal Rock State Wayside, north of Waldport.

for ocean salmon, returning with a catch that ranks behind only the Columbia River area and Winchester Bay. Bottom fishing is popular year-round in the ocean and bay, and from the jetties. Famous Yaquina Bay Dungeness crabs are caught year-round from boats and docks. Clams are abundant, especially during minus tides at Sally's Bend, east of Newport. Commercial fishermen produce large catches of salmon, crab, tuna, shrimp, and bottom fish, and oysters are grown commercially.

Drive along Newport's picturesque bay front, where you'll see docks and moorages for hundreds of boats, charter fishing outfits, a public boat ramp, fish canneries, numerous shops and seafood restaurants. (Try the thick clam chowder at Mo's.) At Undersea Gardens, you can see hundreds of marine creatures through 112 windows 10 feet below the sea, plus a 20-minute scuba diving show each hour; admission is charged. Guided tours of the two-masted wooden sailing schooner "Sara" are offered most afternoons at a nearby wharf for a modest fee.

Drive under the bridge to Yaquina Bay State Park, which has a commanding view out to sea and back into the bay. It's an extremely popular park for picnics and other day uses. It's fun to watch vessels pass under the handsome bridge, ranging from delicate sailboats to huge freighters laden with forest products. Trails descend down the bluff to the beach. The old Yaquina Bay Lighthouse, built in 1871 and abandoned three years later, has been preserved and restored. Marine exhibits are being developed. It's open Thursday through Monday in summer, from 12:30 to 7:30 p.m., and Sunday afternoons in winter; a modest fee is charged. Ask the guide about its legendary ghost.

Other Newport attractions include the Royal Pacific Wax Museum and the Lincoln County Museum. The latter features Indian artifacts, pioneer life and farming, logging and maritime exhibits in a log cabin and nearby home. It's open daily except Monday, from 10-5 in summer and 11-4 in winter.

Consider a side trip east to Toledo, preferably along Bay Road, past the site of old Yaquina City. When the railroad reached here from Corvallis in 1885, Yaquina City became a seaport and boomtown. Toledo's huge Georgia-Pacific mill produces pulp, paper and plywood. Visitors over age 10 can tour the mill Monday through Friday at 10:30 a.m. and 1:30 p.m. from June 15 to Labor Day (except during brief shutdown periods.) Toledo has a public moorage and boat launch, and a golf course. Its parks have a covered swimming pool, tennis courts, playgrounds and picnic facilities. At nearby Olalla Lake you can fish, swim, picnic or camp. From Toledo, you may want to visit Siletz, or popular Moonshine Park northwest of Logsden, or follow Highway 229 down the winding Siletz River to Kernville.

After crossing Yaquina Bay from Newport to South Beach, follow nearly 400,000 annual visitors to the Oregon State University Marine Science Center. You'll enjoy its mounted specimens of marine and shore birds, its 10,000-gallon aquarium, the eight-armed octopus, and the tank where you can handle intertidal creatures. Impressive exhibits explain the tides, formation of estuaries, the continental shelf and fishery resources. Films are shown regularly during the summer. It's open daily, from 10-6 in summer, 10-4 in winter; admission: free.

Oregon Aqua-Foods, (owned by Weyerhaeuser), located next door, is one of Oregon's largest private fish farmers. Millions of salmon are released into the ocean from its rearing ponds. Nearby, you'll see the large new South Beach Marina, with moorage for 540 sports and recreation boats.

South Beach State Park extends along the beach for a mile, just south of the bridge. It has 257 improved campsites, open April to October; for reservations from mid-May to Labor Day, mail your request and $4 advance deposit to the park (P.O. Box 1350, Newport 97365). There's a picnic area, and you can fish from the jetty or dig razor clams.

At Lost Creek State Park, four miles farther south,

you'll have a beautiful oceanfront view while picnicking. There's another nice picnic spot just beyond at Ona Beach State Park, along pretty Beaver Creek.

Tourists have enjoyed the Seal Rock area since the mid-1880's, when a large hotel was constructed here. They came then on the newly-built railroad from Corvallis to Yaquina City, down the bay by boat, then down the beach by team and buggy. An underground lava flow here 14 million years ago created the massive rocks along the beach and an offshore ledge of partially submerged basaltic rock (photo, page 36.) Seals, sea lions and marine birds rest here. Seal Rock State Wayside has picnic facilities and trails above the beach. It's fun to watch breakers crash against the offshore rocks, to inspect the rich tidal pools along the beach, and to climb (cautiously) some of the rocks.

Continue south past Driftwood Beach Wayside to Waldport. It's located on a former Indian burial ground along the south side of Alsea Bay. The Alsea River offers excellent salmon, steelhead and cutthroat trout fishing. Sportsmen also take flounder, perch, crab and clams in the bay. Waldport has a public boat launch, a golf course, and varied tourist facilities. Eckman Slough, two miles east of town, is a popular place for trout fishing, waterskiing and motorboat races. Adjacent W. B. Nelson State Wayside has picnic facilities and a bathing dock.

Governor I. L. Patterson Memorial State Park, a mile south of Waldport, has picnic facilities and a beautiful mile-long beach. Beachside State Park also has a picnic area, plus 60 tent and 20 vehicle campsites, open April through October; for reservations from mid-May to Labor Day, mail your request and $4 advance deposit to the park (P.O. Box 1350, Newport, 97365). At nearby Tillicum Beach, the Forest Service has 58 campsites above the beach, many with beautiful ocean front views.

For further information, contact the Chamber of Commerce in Newport (555 S.W. Coast Highway, telephone 265-2462), Toledo or Waldport.

Yaquina Head Lighthouse, north of Newport.

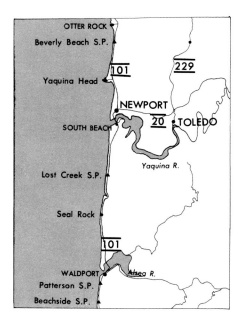

Heceta Head Lighthouse, perhaps the most frequently photographed of all American coastal beacons.

Yachats to Florence

Yachats (say YAH-hots) is perched on a relatively narrow ledge along the sea, with coastal mountains rising up wooded slopes at its back door.

To the south of this quiet seaside village, Highway 101 hugs the shoreline. It winds around or over Cape Perpetua, Heceta Head and other coastal promontories before dropping onto coastal plains and dunes near Florence.

The Indians favored this area, leaving here the coast's greatest concentration of shell mounds, the remains of shellfish they devoured. White settlement developed slowly, until a wagon road was blasted around mighty Cape Perpetua in 1914 and the highway was opened north to Waldport in 1930.

Yachats exudes a quiet charm. Tourists are served by a number of motels, restaurants and shops. Fishermen enjoy success off nearby rocky points and the beaches, and the Yachats River has good steelhead, cutthroat and salmon runs. Silver smelt select the Yachats beaches for annual spawning runs, which usually begin in June and continue through the summer (with occasional runs in spring and fall). Fishermen charge into the surf, dipping nets and

scooping the sardine-like fish into buckets. Thousands are eaten at the Silver Smelt Fry each July. Smelt Sands State Wayside has been developed north of town. Yachats also has a public boat landing, and Yachats State Park is a particularly scenic spot on the rocky point north of the river. The beaches yield clams, agates and jasper, and marine life is abundant in the tidepools here.

Cape Perpetua is the bold, basaltic headland that looms to the south. British navigator James Cook discovered the cape in 1778 and named it for martyred St. Perpetua. Don't miss Siuslaw National Forest's Visitor Center, featuring many exhibits and a fine 15-minute film on the natural forces that shaped this area. Open daily from 9-6 in summer (Wednesdays through Sundays from 10-4 in winter), it attracts more than 130,000 visitors annually.

Drive (or hike) two miles to the top of Cape Perpetua. Take an easy 10-minute walk on the "Trail of the Whispering Spruce" around the 800-foot-high summit. The views are spectacular, north to Cape Foulweather and south (photo, page 4), toward Coos Bay. The cape has picnic facilities, a 37-site campground, and marvelous trails. You can hike to the beach, past spouting horns and tidepools rich with marine life; through towering spruce forests (including one where you can borrow a tape player which explains forest management practices); along sea cliffs, past a shell mound, and to Devil's Churn. The latter (photo, page 39) is a long, narrow, deep fissure in the basalt sea ledge into which mighty waves roll and churn. It's spectacular during a storm. So is Cook's Chasm, a half-mile to the south.

The highway follows the shoreline the next dozen miles. Neptune State Park (photo, page 39) has picnic facilities, a nice beach, and two miles of ocean frontage just south of the cape. At Strawberry Hill, you can often observe seal offshore from the parking area or trail. You can picnic at Ocean Beach or at Ponsler and Carl G. Washburne Memorial State Parks. The latter (donated by the widow of a Eugene businessman and highway commissioner) has two miles of beach, a bathhouse, and sites for 58 trailer and 8 tent campers. The Forest Service also has a nice 16-site campground just above the beach at Rock Creek, a new "bike and hike" campground reached by a quarter-mile trail just south of the Rock Creek bridge, and more primitive campsites about six miles up both Tenmile and Big Creeks.

Heceta Head (say Ha-SEA-ta) was named for Spanish navigator Bruno Heceta. Its remarkable natural beauty was enhanced by construction of a lighthouse in 1894 (photo, cover and page 38). One of the most photographed lighthouses in America, you'll want to shoot from the south. There's a lovely view from Devil's Elbow State Park, a popular beach, picnic and surf fishing spot nestled in the secluded cove between Cape Creek and the headland. A trail leads up from the beach about a half-mile to the lighthouse, offering spectacular views.

Sea Lion Caves, a mile south of Heceta Head, hosts the only known year-round colony of Steller sea lions anywhere on the U.S. mainland. The mighty Pacific

Above: Devil's Churn can be spectacular when a stormy sea drives big waves into narrow fissure.

Below: Mighty Cape Perpetua shields Neptune State Park from the northerly winds of summer.

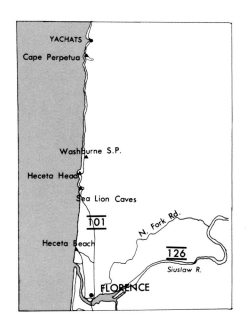

has carved here America's largest sea cave, with a 125-foot-high dome and two-acre floor that's washed constantly by the surging surf. An average of 250 sea lions live here in the area. After wintering in the cave, they move out onto nearby sea ledges as the weather improves and the sea calms in spring. After the breeding season of late spring and early summer, they begin gradually moving back to the cave. Numerous sea birds also nest here on the cliffs and off shore islands, including gulls, pigeon guillemot, brown pelicans, and reportedly North America's largest concentration of nesting cormorants.

Unlike the Alaska fur seal, these sea lions have no commercial value. They are air-breathing mammals that eat fish they catch themselves. Bulls, about twice the size of the cows, weigh an average of about 1,500 pounds. A few of the largest bulls attract and fiercely defend harems of more than a dozen cows each through the spring breeding season, after which the breeding bulls disappear for the winter.

The cave was discovered in 1880 by a local seaman, who bought the property from the state. It was opened to the public in 1932, shortly after the newly graveled coast highway made the area accessible. Three families (Houghton, Jacobson and Saubert) have jointly owned the cave for more than 40 years. Its popularity grew slowly until the 208-foot elevator was opened in 1961. Now about 200,000 people visit annually. Admission is charged to visit the cave.

South of Sea Lion Caves, the highway winds down off the high seafront bluffs. There's a fine view of the beach and Lily Lake from roadside turnouts. The highway veers inland, behind the first of the great dunes which line the coast for 50 miles, past several pretty lakes and four Forest Service campgrounds. Two are at Alder and nearby Dune Lakes, with 39 trailer sites and nice trails around the lakes and up into the dunes to the west. Others are at Sutton Lake (boat ramp, picnic facilities, and sites for 11 tents and 19 trailers) and at Sutton Creek (3 tents, 60 trailers.)

Darlingtonia State Wayside has picnic facilities. It features a view from a short loop trail of the rare Californica Darlingtonia (cobra-lily), which traps and digests insects. Mercer Lake, a mile east, has trout to match its beauty, plus a public boat landing.

If you aren't in a hurry, proceed to Florence via the beach loop. Turn west to Heceta Beach, where there's a county park. Then drive south along the beach and lower Siuslaw River to Siuslaw Harbor Vista County Park. It's a nice place to picnic or to fish off the north jetty. Rhododendrons line this route and bloom in gorgeous pink in May or early June.

Florence has many motels, restaurants, a golf course and tourist-oriented businesses. A number of interesting shops have been opened in its "Old Town" section along the bay, under the bridge. It's the northern gateway to the Oregon Dunes National Recreation Area, described on pages 41-45. It's also a great place for fishermen, with temptations that include charter boat trips to sea, the Siuslaw River, and many nearby lakes. The lower Siuslaw is famed for its sea-run cutthroat trout and also is an excellent salmon and steelhead stream.

If you have time for an inland side trip, try the scenic 35-mile loop up the North Fork, over Neely Mountain to Mapleton, then down the Siuslaw on Highway 126 to Florence.

More information about Cape Perpetua may be obtained from the Siuslaw National Forest's Waldport Ranger Station. For more information about western Lane County tourist attractions, contact the Florence Chamber of Commerce, P.O. Box 712, telephone 997-3128.

Hundreds of sea lions inhabit America's largest ocean cavern, Sea Lion Caves, north of Florence. A modern elevator takes visitors down near sea level, where you can observe these mammals.

The Oregon Dunes

Sunbathing, swimming, sailing and strolling at pretty Cleawox Lake.

North America's most spectacular coastal sand dunes line the shore from Florence south to Coos Bay.

Wind-blown sand from the sea keeps marching inland in a relentless tide, around and sometimes over shorepine and other lush native vegetation.

Hike into these dunes and you'll discover another world, one of total solitude. Undulating, wind-sculpted sand and soft shadows stretch to the horizon. But this isn't a desert. With annual precipitation of nearly 70 inches, it's a natural rain forest that has been invaded by alien sand.

Why is the sand so abundant here? Geologists explain that most Oregon coastal mountains consist primarily of tough volcanic rock. But sandstone and other soft sedimentary deposits predominate east of the dunes. They erode easily, so the streams carry billions of grains of sand to the sea. Ocean currents sweep this sand onto the beach, where the prevailing westerly winds blow it inland.

These are called "living dunes," because the sand continues to advance eastward an average of three to four feet each year. But man's tinkering with nature in recent decades threatens the future of these dunes. European beach grass was planted near the mouths of navigable rivers to stabilize the sand and prevent it from plugging river channels. This plant has spread since the 1930s up and down the coast. Such grasses above the beach deflect the wind upward, causing sand to drop at their feet. The result has been the buildup of foredunes up to 25 feet high just above the high tide line. They constitute a barrier that has drastically reduced the movement of sand inland. Some experts believe that unless the foredunes are removed these "living dunes" are doomed to stabilization within the next century or two, in which case native vegetation would cover the dunes.

The low, flat area behind the foredune is the deflation plain. The wind often blows away everything down to the moist sand near the water table, which explains the heavy vegetation there. This plain is moving eastward at a rate of 10 to 15 feet per year.

Small transverse dunes are found just above the plain. Their ridges are at right angles to the northwesterly winds in summer. In winter, they turn perpendicular to the southwesterly winds.

Then, marching inland, the sand rises into the mighty oblique dunes unique to this area. They frequently rise 300 feet or more above sea level. They line up in a series of ridges, several hundred feet apart, parallel to the beach and each other at an oblique angle to the prevailing summer and winter winds. At the upper end you find the "zone of confrontation," where advancing sand slides down the eastern or lee slope in tiny avalanches, burying everything in its path.

Several dozen freshwater lakes enhance this area. Some are within the dunes, where the sand holds the heavy winter rainfall like a sponge. Others were formed where advancing dunes trapped upland streams. These lakes offer exceptional fishing, as well as boating, swimming and other water sports. Numerous campgrounds and picnic areas beckon visitors. Forests of spruce, fir and hemlock shield more than 400 species of wildlife. Add the beaches, dunebuggy fun, and additional fishing in the ocean and nearby streams and you have a vacation paradise.

Congress recognized this area's unique attributes when it created the Oregon Dunes National Recreation Area in 1972. Siuslaw National Forest manages this 50-square-mile area, which extends down the coast nearly 40 miles from the Siuslaw River almost to Coos Bay.

Florence (page 40) is the area's northern gateway.

Your first good access to the dunes is via South Jetty Road, one mile south of Florence. It takes you west over the dunes less than two miles to the beach and the first of seven parking lots. Then it turns north, just behind the foredunes, continuing nearly four miles to the jetty, where you can fish for perch and rockfish.

Honeyman State Park has it all—two beautiful lakes for swimming, sunbathing, boating and fishing; lush forests which provide an umbrella for campgrounds, trails and lakeside picnic areas; and more of those mighty dunes.

Charming Cleawox Lake has a picnic and swimming area on the northeast shore, complete with bathhouse, floating dock and lifeguards. But the popular south shore attracts even more bathers, with deep white sand that drops down steep slopes into the pretty lake (photo, page 41.) Kids (of all ages) have a marvelous time racing down the dunes, sometimes tumbling and rolling in the sand. Others slide on platters (photo, page 43.)

You can hike over those high dunes west of Cleawox (photo, page 42) more than a mile to the beach. But it's slow going in the deep sand. Hiking trails lead around the east side of the lake, and around nearby Lily Lake, to the campground. It's open year-round, with 241 tent sites, 75 improved sites and 66 sites with full utility hookups; for reservations from mid-May to Labor Day, mail your request and $4 advance deposit to the park (84505 Hwy - 101, Florence 97439).

Honeyman State Park also borders the north end of

Hikers ascend the mighty dunes west of Honeyman State Park.

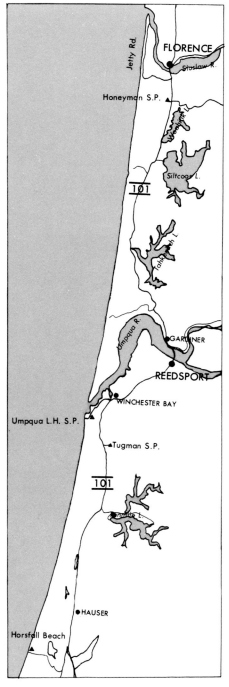

Woahink Lake, east of Highway 101. It's also a popular place for swimming (beach and bathhouse), boating (two ramps), waterskiing and picnicking (photo, page 43.)

You'll see a commercial dunebuggy operation at Dunes City, one mile south of Honeyman. Drivers will take you on exciting rides over the dunes. The buggies charge over the ridges and then down steep banks, with occasional backward slides. Admission is charged.

Siltcoos Lake, the area's largest, lies east of the highway south of Woahink. Turn east a quarter-mile to the resort village of Westlake. Siltcoos Lake is famed for its largemouth bass fishing and also yields fine catches of catfish, perch, crappies and itinerant cutthroat and salmon. Tyee Forest Camp has 14 tent sites and a boat launch, and there's also a county ramp at Westlake.

One mile south, turn west to the Siltcoos River Recreation Area and the beach. Forest Service campgrounds provide 99 regular campsites, plus 90 others in a campground designed for users of off-road vehicles. You can hike (or dunebuggy) into the dunes, or along the beach. Silver salmon and cutthroat are caught in the river.

Dunebuggies and other off-road vehicles congregate here, as well as in the area south of South Jetty Road, the area south of Umpqua Lighthouse State Park, and the area north of Horsfall Road. These vehicles come in many shapes and sizes, equipped with very wide, underinflated tires for sand traction. Large areas are open to off-road vehicles, while others are closed either seasonally or year-round. Drivers should pick up the off-road vehicles regulations and map from the NRA office in Reedsport.

Carter Lake is long and narrow, surrounded by dunes. There's a picnic area on the east shore and a boat launch, used by trout fishermen. The campground on the west shore has 22 sites, plus more picnic tables.

Fishermen catch rainbow and cutthroat trout in Lost and Elbow Lakes, south of Carter Lake. Crown Zellerbach Corp. has provided public campgrounds and picnic areas at both lakes, but the road into Elbow Lake has been washed out.

Tahkenitch Lake, 13 miles south of Florence, is another popular place for fishing, swimming, and other water sports. It's second only to Siltcoos Lake as a producer of bass, yellow perch, catfish, rainbow trout, bluegills, salmon and steelhead. There's a campground with 36 tent and trailer sites, plus boat

Above: Swimming, picnicking, boating and water-skiing are popular at Woahink Lake. Below: It's fun to slide or race down dunes at Cleawox Lake.

43

Lush forests surround Tenmile Lake,

a popular place for fishing and boating.

launch and picnic area. A delightful trail leaves the southwest corner of the campground and takes you a half-mile through old-growth forest that's being invaded by sand. You'll get a fine view of dunes and ocean from the end of this trail, and you can proceed across the dunes less than a mile to the beach. Or, just north of the highway bridge, you can cross the dam over Tahkenitch Creek and hike across the dunes to the ocean.

You can drive four rough miles almost to the beach on Road 247, four miles south of Tahkenitch. You also may want to hike over the dunes to secluded Threemile Lake, nestled between dunes about a mile north of this road and a half-mile inland from the beach. A narrow corridor has been provided off-road vehicles, down the beach and then back across the Umpqua spit to a popular spot for clamming and duck hunting.

Gardiner and Reedsport are on opposite banks of the broad Umpqua River. Gardiner and Scottsburg, 16 miles upstream, were the leading settlements in

Dunebuggies, with flags flying, are ready to

roll up and over massive dunes near Florence.

pioneer times. But Reedsport has become the major center for trade and tourist facilities. The Umpqua attracts fishermen by the thousands. It's noted for salmon (spring, as well as fall) and steelhead (summer, as well as winter.) It's also a fine stream for cutthroat, striped bass, sturgeon and shad. Crabbing and clamming are popular in the bay.

While in Reedsport, stop at the National Recreation Area Visitor Center, just west of the junction of Highways 101 and 38. Fine displays and helpful staff explain the area's natural wonders.

If you're ready for a side trip, there's a lovely drive up the Umpqua, past a state wayside with boat launch and picnic tables, to Scottsburg. You can turn south off Highway 38 seven miles to Loon Lake, where there's excellent trout fishing and a large BLM campground and picnic area. The drive up the winding Smith River from Gardiner is another pleasant one.

Winchester Bay, four miles south of Reedsport, is a mecca for ocean fishermen. Nearly 1,200 sports and commercial fishing boats are moored at Salmon Harbor, which also has restaurants, motels and a custom fish cannery. It claims to be Oregon's leading sports fishing harbor, and ranks behind only the Astoria area, Coos Bay and Newport in commercial fishing. But the bottom fishing here doesn't equal the salmon fishing. So there's a plan to build an artificial reef out of used tires about two miles offshore to attract flounder, sea bass and halibut. Adjacent Windy Cove County Park has 20 tent and 50 trailer campsites, plus picnic facilities, a bathhouse and a playground. A nearby road leads along the bay past Ziolkouski Beach County Park to the jetty, where it connects with the adjacent state park.

Umpqua Lighthouse State Park, just south of Winchester Bay, has varied attractions. The lighthouse, constructed in 1893, isn't open to the public. But there's a new county museum (open Wednesdays through Sundays in summer) that features marine and timber exhibits. Nearby Lake Marie (photo, page 45) is a three-acre jewel surrounded by spruce, hemlock and rhododendrons. Take the delightful trail around the lake. There's a nice picnic area and a nearby campground, open April through October, with 41 tent and 22 trailer sites. The road past the lighthouse leads to the jetty, a popular fishing spot, and then about two miles south along the beach. You can hike here into dunes that are among the highest in the U.S., rising to an elevation of 545 feet west of Clear Lake.

Tugman State Park is located on the west shore of Eel Lake, eight miles south of Reedsport. It has 115 improved campsites, a swimming beach, bathhouse and large picnic area. Trout fishermen use a boat launch. The Forest Service has another large camp one mile south at Eel Creek, with 78 sites. A short trail from the parking area leads into the dunes at their widest point, where you can hike 2½ miles over the sand to the ocean.

Tenmile Lakes attract numerous visitors for fishing, swimming, sailing, canoeing, motorboating and water-skiing. Lakeside, a mile east of the highway on the **shores of North and South Tenmile Lakes, has varied tourist facilities. The lakes are beautiful (photo, page 44),** with 178 miles of shoreline bordering long arms that reach deep into lush forests. They are best known for bass, catfish and bluegill fishing, but also yield good catches of rainbow and cutthroat trout. The Coos Bay Yacht Club stages colorful Sunday afternoon sailboat races here.

The highway passes to the east of several small lakes south of Lakeside. Many are inaccessible by automobile. An exception is Saunders Lake, with a public boat landing and good trout fishing.

To reach Horsfall Beach, turn west in the middle of Haynes Inlet, a northern arm of Coos Bay. The road leads to the beach and to high dunes, including areas used by dunebuggies and other off-road vehicles. A Forest Service camp at Bluebill Lake has 19 trailer sites and a nice mile-long trail that skirts the edge of the lake.

For further information about this area, contact the Oregon Dunes National Recreation Area, 855 Highway Ave., Reedsport 97467, telephone 271-3611, or the Chamber of Commerce at Reedsport, Florence, Coos Bay, North Bend, or Lakeside.

Above: Lovely Lake Marie, in Umpqua Lighthouse State Park. Below: A typical scene in Oregon Dunes National Recreation Area.

Handsome sandstone sea cliffs face the thundering Pacific at Shore Acres State Park.

Around Coos Bay

Shore Acres State Park also features colorful formal and Oriental gardens.

The Coos Bay area can claim many distinctions — the world's largest forest products shipping port; the largest bay and best natural harbor between San Francisco and the Columbia River; and the Oregon Coast's largest population center.

It's rich in tourist attractions, too, including several outstanding state parks and excellent sports fishing.

You'll cross the bay into North Bend on the mile-long C. B. McCullough Bridge, over arches that rise nearly 150 feet over the main channel to permit the passage of huge cargo ships. McCullough supervised the design of many Oregon highway bridges. They include this one, constructed in 1936, and equally impressive coastal spans at Newport and Gold Beach.

Originally the home of the Coos Indians, white settlers began arriving here in the 1850's. They started cutting and shipping timber almost immediately, enterprises that continue to dominate the local economy.

Driving through North Bend and Coos Bay, you'll see at least seven very large lumber, plywood and pulp mills. They produce most of the more than $550 million worth of forest products shipped from this port annually. All of the wood chips (photo, page 47) and about 80 per cent of the total are sent to Japan. Ocean-going freighters use a channel that has been dredged 35 feet deep and 300 feet wide. It extends 15 miles from the mouth of the bay past 13 deepwater docks and three big turning basins.

Oregon's second largest commercial fishery centers at Charleston, just inside the mouth of the bay on South Slough. Six plants there can or cold-pack annually more than a million dollars worth of salmon, tuna, other fish, shrimp and crab. Several firms at nearby Barview grow oysters from imported seed.

Drive west from North Bend or Coos Bay to Empire and then down the lower bay to Charleston, en route to three outstanding state parks. About 600 commercial and sports fishing boats are moored in the Charleston boat basin, surrounded by motel, restaurants, trailer park, boat launch, tackle shops, boat works and seafoods processors. Charter boats and private craft go over the bar for salmon and a wide variety of bottom fish. Abundant catches of striped bass, shad, steelhead and cutthroat trout are taken from the bay and the Coos and Millicoma Rivers. The crabbing also is excellent in the bay, and rock and jetty fishermen take many perch and ling cod. While in Charleston, you may tour the U.S. Coast Guard Station most afternoons. The University of Oregon Institute of Marine Biology is here, near the 4,500-acre state estuarine sanctuary recently created along South Slough.

Bastendorff County Park is two miles west of Charleston, on the way to the state parks. It has a picnic area, restrooms, and campsites for 30 tents and 25 trailers. A road winds down the hill to the beach. It extends north to the south jetty, a popular fishing spot, and is known for razor clams.

Oregon wood chips, bound for Japan.

The main road continues south past Cape Arago Lighthouse (closed to the public) to Sunset Bay State Park (photo, page 47.) It overlooks a beautiful bay, which nestles in a small cove between steep sandstone bluffs. With a narrow opening to the sea, this shallow bay offers one of the safest places on the coast to surf bathe and (on incoming tides) to swim. Sunset Bay also attracts surfers, skin divers and boatsmen, who launch small craft into the surf at the north end of the sandy beach. There's a bathhouse and a picnic area just above the beach. The campground, open April through October, has 108 tent sites and 29 more with full utilities; for reservations from mid-May to Labor Day, mail your request and $4 advance deposit to the park (Route 2, Box 738, Coos Bay 97420).

One of three Coos Bay area golf courses is located next to the park. The others are Coos Country Club, south of Coos Bay, and Kentuck Golf Club, east of the bay.

Most visitors drive from Sunset Bay to two nearby state parks. But the best way to see this beautiful oceanfront is from a newly-developed 3½-mile hiking trail. It starts near the Sunset Bay picnic area and follows coastline bluffs past Shore Acres State Park to the roadside viewpoint north of Cape Arago.

Shore Acres State Park combines spectacular oceanfront scenery and beautiful formal and Oriental gardens. It's located just south of Sunset Bay on the former estate of lumber and shipping magnate Louis J. Simpson. He sold 637 acres to the state in 1942 for just $29,000, including a 224-foot-long mansion and botanical gardens with more than 3,000 plants. The Simpsons previously donated the land occupied by Cape Arago State Park and Simpson Park in North Bend.

Follow the paved path that winds under towering Sitka spruce and along the seafront. Those splendid 50-foot-high sandstone cliffs (photo, page 46) have absorbed the pounding of the surf for millions of years. Some of the sedimentary slabs have been undermined and now tilt at a 45-degree angle. Winter storms drive waves and froth high in the air here in a spectacular show. You can watch one comfortably from the glass-enclosed observation shelter which stands on the site of the former Simpson mansion.

The formal garden, recently restored by the state

(photo, page 46), has concrete walkways, boxwood hedges, and beautiful annuals and perennials. Many of the original plants were imported by Simpson from far corners of the world on lumber schooners built at his North Bend shipyard. The state also has renovated his adjoining Japanese garden. A 100-foot-wide lily pond is surrounded by abundant fuchsias, ferns and bamboo, plus stone lanterns and other decorative features. The park also has a small picnic area, and a trail leads down to a pleasant, secluded beach.

Cape Arago State Park is less than a mile further south, at the western tip of the cape. Stop en route at a roadside viewpoint, where you can see and hear sea lions and sea birds on Simpson Reef. It's a sandstone shelf that tilts westward a half-mile offshore. Big breakers crash across the reef, creating wild wave action. The park, at the end of the road, offers marvelous views up and down the coastline. Some picnic tables are in the open, while others are screened by spruce and thick salal. Steep trails descend to coves north and south of the point. The latter beach is known for its agates. Small pleasure boats often anchor here, protected by the cape from northerly winds. It's a popular place to fish off the rocks.

If you're in a hurry to continue down the coast, at Charleston you can turn south on Seven Devil's Road. Several intersecting roads go west to the beach. They

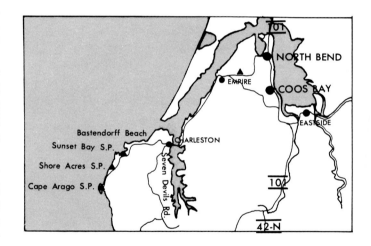

Below: The sandy beach at Sunset Bay State Park.

Above: Silver Falls, one of two pretty cascades in Golden and Silver Falls State Park. Below: Hike to the falls through dense fir forest.

lead to Agate Beach and Whiskey Run, both noted for agates, and to Seven Devil's State Wayside, which has nice picnic facilities. Gold was discovered in beach sand at Whiskey Run in 1852, igniting a mining boom that spread down the coast to Gold Beach, Pistol River, Ophir, Port Orford, Cape Blanco and Bandon.

But there's much to see back in North Bend and Coos Bay.

You can tour Weyerhaeuser's huge forest products mill. From mid-June through August, tours are offered Monday through Friday at 1:30 p.m. (rest of year, Fridays only.) Go to the office along Highway 101.

The Coos-Curry Pioneer Museum, located in North Bend's Simpson Park, displays thousands of interesting items used by local residents since pioneer times, plus splendid Indian artifacts. Note the 14 U.S. flags dating back to 1776. The museum is open daily except Monday, from 11-5 in summer (1-5 on Sunday) and 1-5 p.m. from October through April; admission: free.

Visit a myrtlewood factory, where craftsmen convert the very hard, finely textured wood of a native tree into beautiful plates, trays, bowls and other items. Logs from myrtle trees more than 100 years old are dried for several weeks. Then skilled hands, band-saws and lathes produce roughs of desired items. These roughs are dried for several months before craftsmen put them back on the lathes for turning, sanding and polishing. The beautiful grains of yellow, brown, red and gray are finished with several coats of oil or polyurethane. You can see the entire process at House of Myrtlewood, at the south end of Coos Bay. You'll also pass many smaller myrtlewood factories and shops along the southern coast.

If you have two or three hours to spare, I recommend a 25-mile trip to Golden and Silver Falls State Park. Drive east to Eastside and up the pretty valleys of the Coos and Millicoma Rivers. There's a lovely picnic spot under myrtle trees at a state park along the Millicoma, above Allegany. Pavement gives way to rough gravel the last five miles; incidentally, you can ignore that "Bridge Out" sign.

Two pretty waterfalls tumble down 200-foot-high cliffs in this park, surrounded by a beautiful stand of fir in the canyons of Silver and Glenn Creeks. The parking lot and picnic area (no water) are near the confluence of the creeks. It's an easy quarter-mile walk to Silver Falls (photo, page 48), where Silver Creek spreads out in a lovely spray around a basaltic knob and falls into a pool below. After returning to the parking area, hike a quarter-mile through the woods to Golden Falls, where Glenn Creek plunges over a lava cliff.

For more information, contact the Bay Area Chamber of Commerce, P.O. Box 210, Coos Bay 97420; telephone 269-0215 or 756-4711.

Bandon by-the-sea

Scenic beach and offshore rocks beautify Bandon's oceanfront.

Bandon boasts one of Oregon's most photogenic oceanfronts, thanks to an array of scenic offshore sea stacks of various sizes and shapes.

Bandon also is noted for cranberries and cheddar, and for rebounding twice in this century from disastrous fires. The 1936 holocaust destroyed nearly every building in town.

It's a small seaport near the mouth of the pretty Coquille River, used by ocean-going barges to carry lumber from upstream mills. Bandon is among the state's 10 largest commercial fishing ports, with salmon, tuna, halibut, snappers and shrimp leading the way. The Coquille River also attracts numerous sports fishermen, particularly for fine steelhead and cutthroat runs. Anglers also catch salmon, striped bass and shad. Crab are taken in the lower river and clams in the tide flats.

Bullard's Beach State Park covers nearly two square miles of dunes and woods just north of Bandon and the river. Four miles of beach extend along the ocean and river. There's a pleasant picnic area near the riverside boat ramp. The campground has 100 improved sites, plus 92 more for trailers with full utilities.

The Coquille River Lighthouse, near Bandon.

It's open year-round. You can tour the park's rehabilitated but unfurnished Coquille River Lighthouse (photo below). Constructed in 1896, it was abandoned in the 1930's.

Highway 101 follows an inland path for more than 50 miles between Coos Bay and Port Orford. Leave the highway in Bandon and take the Beach Loop four miles south down the scenic seafront. You can turn west at 1st Street, and drive past the harbor and the jetty, or at 11th Street. The Beach Loop passes Table Rock, Coquille Point, Face Rock, Bandon Ocean Wayside, Bandon State Park and Bradley Lake.

The offshore rock formations are beautiful. Stroll along the sandy, uncrowded beach, whether you're looking for pictures, agates or driftwood. Bring plenty of film, and return with more at sunset. The state park has a nice picnic area (no water) and interesting dunes. You'll find good trout fishing and a boat ramp at Bradley Lake, which is protected from ocean winds by high dunes.

Bandon is known as Oregon's cranberry capital. You'll see large bogs north and south of town, covered with thick, reddish, low-growing vines. The red berries are harvested in October. One local firm makes and sells many kinds of cranberry candy. There's a Cranberry Festival each September.

Oregon's second largest cheese factory (680 Highway 101) invites visitors every day except Sunday from 8-5. You can watch the making of fine cheddar through observation windows during morning hours. Narrated color slides explain the process.

Other Bandon area attractions include beaches northwest of the city, off Seven Devils Road (see page 48); the wetlands north of Bandon between the river and highway, temporary home of thousands of migratory birds; the state fish hatchery, just east of town; and a historical museum in the downtown area.

For further information, write the Chamber of Commerce, P. O. Box 1115.

Port Orford

Battle Rock and Port Orford beach, looking toward Humbug Mountain.

Highway 101 returns to the coast at picturesque Port Orford, after following an inland path for more than 50 miles south from Coos Bay.

You may choose interesting side trips to Floras Lake, Cape Blanco, or up the Elk or Sixes Rivers. At Port Orford, you'll begin a spectacular 15-mile oceanfront drive past Humbug Mountain, Lookout Rock and Sisters Rocks.

Floras Lake, near Langlois, is a popular place to sail, waterski, and to fish for trout or bass. Boicope County Park has a campground, picnic area and boat ramp. Floras Lake was the site of Pacific City, launched in 1908 by real estate promoters who promised development of a great seaport here by cutting a channel to the ocean. They platted 6,000 lots and attracted hundreds of residents and many businesses (including a hotel, sawmill and weekly newspaper.) But the channel wasn't feasible, for the lake is 40 feet above sea level and would have been drained. Disillusioned residents all moved away within a few years, and the forest has overgrown the townsite.

Cape Blanco, a few miles to the south, is the westernmost point in Oregon. Navigator Martin D'Aguilar noted its chalky (fossilized sea shells) cliffs in 1603 and named it "White Cape" in Spanish. Its lighthouse (photo, page 51), built in 1870, is Oregon's oldest still in use. Despite its million-candlepower beam seen 22 miles at sea, many vessels and dozens of lives have been lost in the treacherous waters below. The Coast Guard also operates a Loran Station here, which sends a powerful radiobeam 250 miles to guide mariners and pilots.

The adjacent Cape Blanco State Park covers about three square miles on the former Patrick Hughes ranch. It has 58 improved campsites (open mid-April through October), a picnic area, and a boat launch along the Sixes River. Trails lead to several beaches about 200 feet below the cape, where visitors enjoy surf fishing, beachcombing and clamming.

The Sixes River attracts salmon and steelhead fishermen. You can drive up the north bank a few miles to Edson Creek County Park and a B.L.M. campground.

Elk River, just south of the cape, provides excellent fishing for fall salmon, winter steelhead and cutthroat trout. The south bank road is paved seven miles to the state fish hatchery, which welcomes visitors, and continues over gravel to two Forest Service campgrounds.

Port Orford enjoys a particularly scenic setting, overlooking a pretty, deep-water bay just south of a promontory called "The Heads." The westernmost city in the 48 contiguous states, it was Curry County's first white settlement and first county seat.

Sea Capt. William Tichenor envisioned a profitable trading post here. So in 1851 he recruited nine men and left them here on one of his regular Portland-San Francisco voyages. Noting Indians along the beach, the men took the ship's cannon and small arms ashore. They set up camp atop the large basaltic rock that rises from the sand, pointing the cannon down its backbone toward the beach. This enabled them to repulse two fierce attacks by several dozen Indians. But Tichenor's ship did not return on schedule two weeks later. With food and ammunition running low, the men escaped to the north one dark night. Later that summer, Tichenor returned with 67 well-armed men. They built a trading post that was used as an army base during the Rogue Indian War, which ended in 1856 when the government shipped hundreds of natives to the Siletz Indian Reservation.

Visit Battle Rock State Wayside, below the highway at the south edge of Port Orford. There's a delightful beach, and a beautiful view south past offshore rocks to Humbug Mountain (photo, page 50) and northwest into the harbor. It's fun to climb the historic rock;

note the graves of one of its defenders, his wife and son.

Drive around to the harbor, where numerous commercial and sports fishermen return with salmon, shrimp, ling cod, snapper, crab and tuna. A large hoist lifts fishing boats between the dock and the ocean. Go up W. 9th Street to The Heads, where there's another state park and marvelous coastal views to the north and south. Then drive out 14th or 18th Streets to Garrison Lake, which has two boat ramps and excellent trout fishing, boating and waterskiing. Buffington City Park has a dock for fishing or swimming along the lake, plus a picnic area, playground, tennis courts, hiking trails, public horse arena and sports field. Popular Paradise Point, just north of the lake, has a beach known for its agates.

There's a beautiful ocean front drive from Port Orford south to Humbug Mountain. The highway rounds Rocky Point, a good place to dig clams. Humbug Mountain seems to sweep up out of the sea. At 1,756 feet, it's the Oregon Coast's second highest peak (slightly below Cascade Head's 1,770, and above Neahkahnie Mountain's 1,710.) You'll swing inland around the mountain, winding up the narrow canyon of Brush Creek.

Humbug Mountain State Park has four miles of coastline. There's a pleasant picnic area along the pretty creek. The campground (open mid-April through October) has 75 tent sites, plus 30 with full utilities. A trail winds three miles up the mountain to the summit, which yields a dramatic view to the south. Or you can hike (or bike) four miles north from the campground, along the former highway route. Fishermen take trout from the stream and striped bass from the nice beach at the mouth of the creek.

Highway 101 follows the scenic shoreline south past Lookout Rock, a massive basaltic cone that rises 568 feet from the sea. You'll pass Arizona Beach, where there's a popular resort and campground. At the nearby Prehistoric Gardens, you can stroll through a lush rain forest past numerous life-sized replicas of

Above: Cape Blanco Lighthouse warns mariners they are nearing Oregon's westernmost point.

Below: The view north to Sisters Rocks.

ancient reptiles; admission is charged.

Sisters Rocks (photo, page 51) beautify the seafront to the south. Look for profiles of three sisters in two large mainland rocks and an offshore island. The cove south of the rocks (Frankport) was used by pioneers as a port to ship out hides and tanoak bark, and as recently as the 1950's as a lumber port.

Ophir (rhymes with gopher) is a rural community in the pretty valley of Euchre Creek. It's one of several Curry County streams that gets plugged at the mouth with sand during low-flow periods. Stream water then backs up in a lagoon, until an increased flow breaks through the sand into the sea. This also is characteristic of the Elk, Sixes, New, Pistol and Winchuck Rivers and of Hunter and Euchre Creeks.

Curry County's only golf course, Cedar Bend, is near Ophir. And Ophir State Wayside has picnic and other day-use facilities along the beach.

For further information, write the Chamber of Commerce, P.O. Box 637, Port Orford 97465.

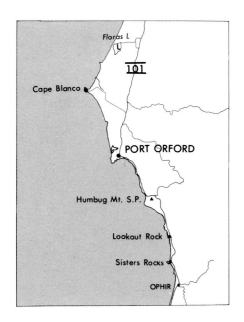

Gold Beach

From Cape Sebastian, there's a sweeping view south to Crook Point.

Gold Beach has the largest concentration of tourist facilities on Oregon's southern coast, including about 400 motel rooms and perhaps a dozen restaurants.

Fishermen flock here for salmon and steelhead angling in the world-renowned Rogue River. Popular jet-boat trips up the river and outstanding coastal scenery attract numerous other tourists.

Approaching Gold Beach from the north, you'll drive past quiet Nesika Beach and Geisel Monument State Wayside, which has picnic facilities. Pioneer John Geisel and his three young sons were killed here in 1856 by Indians angered by the invasion of gold miners and other whites. When the so-called Rogue Indian War ended later that year, the government shipped about 600 natives to the new Siletz Indian Reservation in present Lincoln County.

At nearby Otter Point State Wayside, you can enjoy scenic marine vistas or take the trail down to Agate Beach.

Wedderburn, on the north bank of the Rogue, was named by pioneer R. D. Hume for his ancestral home in Scotland. Hume almost completely dominated Wedderburn and Gold Beach for more than 20 years prior to his death in 1908. He owned the land fronting

The rugged shoreline near Whiskey Creek.

both banks of the river and the ocean, the salmon cannery, large timber holdings and a sawmill, a huge ranch, commercial fishing boats and ocean freighters, the weekly newspaper, boat works, general store and a private race track.

The Rogue is the answer to most fishermen's dreams. You may see dozens of fishing boats on the lower river as you cross the handsome bridge into Gold Beach (photo, page 55.) Nearly 100,000 salmon and steelhead migrate up the Rogue to gravel spawning beds annually. Thousands of 20-30-pound spring chinook enter the river from early April to mid-June. Cutthroat also are caught in spring. The summer steelhead run begins in August and continues for about two months, providing exciting challenges for fishermen and perhaps the finest sports fish of its size in the world. The fall cutthroat migrate upstream at about the same time. Then the first heavy fall rains attract thousands of fall chinook into the river. Finally, from November until March, anglers seek the winter steelhead.

Gold Beach also is a popular place for ocean fishing. Charter boats pursue offshore salmon from June through October, plus varied bottom fish over a longer season. Two-hour scenic cruises are offered. Sports and commercial fishing boats are moored at the port docks, near a seafoods cannery and shrimp plant. Other anglers catch ling cod, perch and sea bass off rocky points, the jetties north and south of the river, or the beach.

Gold Beach is the county seat of Curry County. Miners found gold here in the early 1850's, on the beach, at the mouth of the Rogue, and at Pistol River, Ophir, Port Orford, Cape Blanco, Bandon and Whiskey Run.

While in Gold Beach, don't miss one of those exciting boat trips up the Rogue, described on page 54. Drive up Caughell Street to the city park, which has picnic facilities, tennis courts, playground equipment, a physical fitness trail, and volleyball and softball fields. The Curry County Historical Museum has attractive exhibits on Indian and pioneer life, early mining, fishing, logging and agriculture. Located at the county fairgrounds at the south edge of town, it's open daily except Monday in summer, from 11-5, and Friday through Sunday from 1-5 p.m. from October through April. Admission: free.

The 28-mile drive from Gold Beach to Brookings is the most spectacular on the entire Oregon Coast.

There's easy access to a nice beach at Hunter Creek, at the foot of Kissing Rock, two miles south of Gold Beach. The creek (photo, page 53) often gets plugged by buildup of a sand ridge at its mouth. Fishermen catch some steelhead, fall chinook and cutthroat off the bank. You can drive up the creek into the mountains, then loop back to the highway along either the Rogue or Pistol Rivers. Maps at the Gold Beach Ranger Station show locations of four Forest Service picnic or campground facilities.

The highway climbs south of Hunter Creek, winding in graceful curves along the sides of mountains that rise from the beach. Cape Sebastian, six miles south of Gold Beach, stands more than 700 feet above the sea. Spanish navigator Vizciano Sebastion discovered the headland in 1603 and named it for that day's patron saint, San Sebastian. Drive up the steep side road to the southerly parking area of Cape Sebastian State Park. Hike up the trail a short distance for the best views, south 50 miles to Point St. George (photo, page 52) and north across rugged oceanfront bluffs more than 40 miles to Cape Blanco. The trail winds down the south side of the cape for about two miles to the shoreline.

The highway descends the cape's south slope, returning to the beach north of Myers Creek. A forest of picturesque sea stacks rises from the ocean floor here (photo, page 53.) At low tide, you can reach those nearest the shore, explore surrounding tidepools, and seek abundant razor clams.

Hunter Creek dead ends on the beach.

Sandy beaches line the shore south to Crook Point. You'll pass Pistol River, another stream that often plugs with sand, creating a lagoon that extends about a mile north between the beach and highway. This was the site of a major battle in 1856. Indians surrounded and besieged 34 volunteer soldiers until regulars could rescue them several days later. Curry County's largest sand dunes rise about 100 feet above the beach south of Pistol River. A 440-acre state park extends along the beach and dunes for nearly two miles.

The highway swings east of Crook Point, a 160-foot-high headland south of the dunes. There's a marvelous view from the south side of this point, over impressive 325-foot-high Mack Arch and Mack Reef to Cape Ferrelo. Unfortunately, there's only a very limited view of the handsome arch from the highway. To fully appreciate its grandeur, you need permission to enter private ranches.

For more information about the Gold Beach-Wedderburn area, contact the Chamber of Commerce, P.O. Box 55, Gold Beach 97444, telephone 247-7526.

Sea stacks rise from sandy beach at Myers Creek.

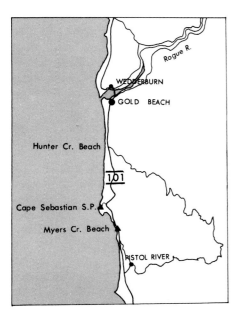

A hydro-jet climbs Clay Hill Rapids on the Rogue—Blackburn photo.

Up the Rogue

Interrupt your drive along Curry County's spectacular coastline long enough for a cruise up the Rogue River.

Fishermen know the Rogue as one of the great salmon and steelhead streams of the world (see page 52.) It's equally renowned for the beautiful path it has cut through rugged mountains between Grants Pass and the sea.

To preserve its wilderness character, man's activities along the Rogue have been restricted by both the National Wild and Scenic Rivers Act of 1968 and the Oregon Scenic Waterways Act of 1970. Both laws regulate an 84-mile stretch of river, from Lobster Creek (10 miles above Gold Beach) to the Applegate River. When you explore the Rogue, you'll understand all this concern about natural preservation.

Three firms in Gold Beach and Wedderburn carry an estimated 50,000 people per year up the river by hydro-jet boats. Most passengers take the 64-mile round trip cruise over the riffles to Agness. Others choose a 104-mile round trip journey into the Wild River area, where the canyon gets deeper and steeper, the river rougher and whiter. It's a safe and comfortable ride. The pilot, with public address system, tells stories of gold mining and Indian wars along the river and points out abundant wildlife. You may see deer and bear in the fir and hemlock forests along the banks, otter and beavers in the river, and ospreys, egret and occasionally eagles overhead.

The 64-mile trip involves a cruise past Lobster Creek, through lovely Copper Canyon, and past the mouth of the Illinois River. You'll have lunch at an Agness lodge.

If you can afford the higher fee, take the smaller faster boats 52 miles upstream to Paradise Bar. Constructed in Gold Beach and designed for the Rogue, these vessels can skim over the rocks with just six inches of watery clearance. You leave the last road behind at Illahe and proceed into the Wild River-designated area. Your jet boat will charge over Clay Hill Rapids (photo, page 54) and other challenging whitewater areas, through deep rocky gorges with vertical canyon walls 1,500 feet high. The boats turn back just below Devil's Staircase Rapids and Blossom Bar. Exciting Mule Creek Canyon and Marial lie just beyond. After a sumptuous feast at a secluded fishing lodge, you'll cruise 30 mph down the river and return to the dock before 4 p.m.

Make advance reservations, if possible. Bring a warm coat for the morning chill along the coast, plus sunshade and long sleeves to protect you from inland sunshine.

The trip may whet your appetite for an even greater adventure on the Rogue, floating for several days (or longer) on flat-bottomed boats or rubber rafts through the entire wilderness area. Commercial outfitters in the Grants Pass area conduct such trips. Some are geared primarily for fishermen, while others are for anyone who enjoys scenery, solitude and the challenges of the rushing river. You can take your own craft, except that a permit is required to float the area between Grave Creek and Watson Creek from Memorial Day weekend to Labor Day. You must apply by January for a lottery held each March; write the Galice Ranger District, P. O. Box 1131, Grants Pass 97526.

If you can't explore the Rogue by boat, see some of it by automobile. A modern paved road follows the south bank from Gold Beach to Agness, past campgrounds and picnic areas at Huntley Park, Lobster Creek and Quosatana. It's possible to continue upstream to Illahe, where there's another campground. Or you can circle around to Marial, where a road penetrates the Wild River section.

Beautiful hiking trails have been developed along the Rogue. The Forest Service recently reopened an old trail on the lower river. It begins at the eastern end of North Bank Road above Lobster Creek and follows the river upstream about 12 miles to Agness. A 40-mile trail follows the river's north bank, from Illahe through the Wild River area to Grave Creek. You can sample portions of this trail after driving to Illahe or Marial. Or you could take the 52-mile boat trip to Paradise Bar, then hike through Mule Creek Canyon to Marial or beyond, and return to Gold Beach by boat

Fishing from the jetty and from boats near the mouth of the famous Rogue River, at Gold Beach.

another day. Most hikers prefer spring, when beautiful wildflowers are in bloom, early summer or fall; the canyon gets awfully hot in July and August.

For further information about the lower Rogue River country, contact Siskiyou National Forest (P.O. Box 440, Grants Pass 97526, or its Gold Beach Ranger Station); or the Medford office of the Bureau of Land Management; or the Chamber of Commerce, P.O. Box 55, Gold Beach 97444, telephone 247-7526.

Sunset over the Rogue River—Blackburn photo.

Boardman State Park

Above: From Arch Rock Point you'll enjoy the seascapes both north and south. Below: Arch Rock, part of an ancient sea cave. Below right: At Natural Bridges, the roof collapsed where two sea caves joined.

The most spectacular section of the entire Oregon Coast, appropriately, bears the name Samuel H. Boardman State Park.

One of America's great scenic drives bisects this park, which extends along the rugged shoreline north of Brookings for 11 miles.

The state acquired these 1,473 magnificent seafront acres about 1950. The rugged coastline was almost inaccessible then, more than 10 years before a modern highway would bring thousands of tourists passing this way. Such timely acquisition was characteristic of Boardman, the great founding father of Oregon's nationally recognized state parks system.

Massive bluffs rise hundreds of feet from the Pacific along most of the park's seafront. They are interrupted by deep canyons that have been cut by tiny creeks en route to the ocean. Coves and secluded beaches nestle between headlands at the mouths of these creeks. Sheep graze on steep hillsides above and below the highway. Countless sea stacks and arches stand offshore, rocky remnants of earlier sea cliffs which the pounding surf chewed away over the centuries.

Highway 101 takes you over and around those massive headlands in graceful, sweeping curves, an engineering and esthetic marvel. It crosses huge fills and spans canyons several hundred feet deep. This modern highway was completed in 1962, replacing a 1924-model road that twisted through the hills to the east. Some sections were built at a cost of more than a million dollars per mile, shattering past records for road construction expense.

You'll enter the park just south of Crook Point and Mack Arch. And while you've just passed such scenic standouts as Cape Sebastian and the Myers Creek sea stacks, even grander sights lie ahead.

Arch Rock Point (or Deer Point) is the first of the park's outstanding attractions. Stop at the viewpoint north of the point for the best view of Arch Rock (photo, page 56.) It's the remains of a cave that was carved out by the sea along an earlier coastline. Drive a quarter-mile to the main parking area, and

stroll down the paved path along the outer edges of the point. You'll look down into lovely coves to the north and south (photo, page 56) and offshore to various islands and Arch Rock. Marvelous ocean views can be captured from some of those picnic tables under the towering spruce trees.

The beach south of Arch Rock Point has few equals for either scenery or solitude. You can park along the highway more than a half-mile south of the point and walk down an unmarked old road to the shoreline. Great basaltic rocks rise from the beach to the south, which should be explored at low tide. But hike here with caution, and don't get trapped behind a rocky promontory by a rising tide.

The highway continues south, across the chasms of Miller, Miner and Wridge Creeks to fascinating Natural Bridges Cove (photo, page 56.) A paved trail leads 150 feet down the hill to an observation point. The bridges are remains of an ancient sea cave, the roofs of which collapsed where they intersected.

The scenery is spectacular for the next two miles. The highway takes you over and around ocean-front bluffs and across the canyons of Patrick, House Prairie, Spruce and China Creeks. Stop at the viewpoints to absorb the marvelous seascapes.

Thomas Creek Bridge stretches about 900 feet across a deep canyon etched by another small stream. The steel span, Oregon's highest highway bridge, rests 345 feet above the creek.

Stop at the viewpoint just south of Bruces Bones Creek (photo, page 57) for another splendid view up the coast. Then drive a quarter-mile to the parking lot above Indian Sands Beach. To see this truly unique beach, take the trail at the south end of the parking lot. It's a five-minute walk down a fairly steep grade, through a thick growth of salal and wind-dwarfed spruce. You'll emerge from dense foliage at the upper end of huge dunes. They slope several hundred feet toward the edge of the sea, where cliffs plunge another hundred feet straight into the Pacific. Winds off the ocean have sculpted the sand of this isolated beach into various unusual shapes. A reddish crust

Rugged bluffs and secluded coves near Bruces Bones Creek.

Above: Waves pound against sea cliffs near Whale Head.

Below and right: A seafront arch is one dramatic feature at unique Indian Sands Beach.

caused by iron in the sand adds to the eerie effect. There's a handsome arch along the sea at the south end of the beach (photos, page 58) and a fine view from the heights at the north end. Coastal Indians gathered on this beach frequently, judging by all the shells, arrowheads and other artifacts that have been found here.

After returning to the highway, you'll wind up and around 696-foot-high Whale Head. As you descend its south slope, a side road drops several hundred feet into Whalehead Cove (photo, page 59.) A rugged promontory protects this delightful beach from northerly winds. It's a popular place for beachcombing, picnics, and other beach fun. Rumrunners landed illegal booze here during Prohibition years. In earlier times, miners worked sands at the mouth of Whalehead Creek; some of their equipment still can be found rusting above the beach.

After crossing Bowman Creek, the highway begins a mile-long ascent of Cape Ferrelo. Near its summit, turn up the hill to House Rock Viewpoint. The site of an air raid sentry tower during World War II, it's the highest point along the park's oceanfront. You'll get a sweeping view north to Cape Sebastian (photo, page 59) and south to Point St. George. A large rock offshore bears some resemblance to a dwelling. An impressive monument here honors Boardman.

A mile to the south, park along

the highway and take a 10-minute walk to the tip of Cape Ferrelo. Portuguese pilot Bartholome Ferrelo was a member of the party that identified this headland in 1542, only 50 years after Christopher Columbus discovered America. It was the first known discovery by a white man within Oregon's borders. Walk out across the grassy headland to the point, at the end of a marine terrace 250 feet above the sea. The view is splendid, especially to the south. Several small beaches are tucked between rocky outcroppings below.

The highway descends the south slope of the cape, which is drained by Lone Ranch Creek. Turn down the side road to the pleasant beach (photo, page 59) that's nestled between the cape and the rugged coastline to the south. It's a popular place for picnics, sunbathing, surfbathing and clamming.

When the mineral priceite was discovered here in about 1890, a borax company bought a ranch and launched mining operations. But the deposit was a limited one, so the area soon reverted to sheep range. When Boardman began assembling the pieces of this park in the late 1940's, he noted that about two miles of choice oceanfront was owned by Borax Consolidated, Ltd., of London. He eventually persuaded the British owners to donate their 367-acre tract to the state (subject to any future mineral rights) for park purposes.

Boardman demonstrated the same combination of imagination,

charm and persistence in persuading many others to donate (or sell below market value) choice land for state parks.

A native of Massachusetts, schooled in Wisconsin, Boardman moved to Oregon in 1903. The young civil engineer homesteaded land along the Columbia River, west of Pendleton, at the present city of Boardman. As the state constructed roads across Eastern Oregon, Boardman became vitally interested in roadside beautification. He led volunteer groups which planted thousands of trees along Highway 30 between The Dalles and Ontario. In 1919, he took a job with the highway department. When a new park commission was organized 10 years later, Oregon's answer to Johnny Appleseed was selected the first state parks superintendent.

What a fortunate choice he proved to be. For the next 21 years, he spearheaded development of what many regard as the nation's finest state parks system. He increased state parks acreage from 6,444 in 1929 to 57,195 in 1950, when he reluctantly retired at age 75. About one-third of the acquisitions were by donation, usually inspired by considerable Boardman salesmanship.

Sam Boardman believed deeply that man needs nature for his mental and spiritual well-being. He foresaw the impact of a growing population upon Oregon and the need to set aside choice natural areas for public use.

"Build when your sinews are young," he once said in urging an aggressive parks acquisition policy. "Build before time makes your recreational heritage prohibitive through cost. Husband that which you have; build unto that which you would preserve."

He practiced effectively what he preached so eloquently. He laid the foundation for a great system of state parks.

Those of us who enjoy these parks today owe a great debt of gratitude to Sam Boardman. Future generations of Oregonians will, too.

High, steep oceanfront bluffs limit access to most coastline areas in Boardman State Park. But it's easy to reach popular Lone Ranch Beach, above, and Whale Head Beach, below.

Below: The beauty of Boardman State Park's rugged coastline can be appreciated from House Rock Viewpoint, the highest place along the park's oceanfront. An impressive monument here honors Samuel H. Boardman, who laid the foundation for Oregon's nationally recognized system of state parks.

A delightful place for a picnic, overlooking the sand at Harris Beach State Park.

The Brookings-Harbor area offers a delightful beach park, fine ocean and river fishing, beautiful seascapes, a mild climate in which flowers bloom by the millions, and Oregon's largest coastal population south of Coos Bay.

It's also a good base for short trips to diverse attractions — north to Boardman State Park and the Rogue River; south into California and the Redwood Empire; and east up the Chetco River, past myrtle-wood and redwood groves to the edge of the rugged Kalmiopsis Wilderness Area.

The lovely four-mile coastline from Boardman State

Brookings

View north over Harris Creek at Harris Beach S.P.

Park south to Brookings features a series of scenic points, coves, beaches, and offshore sea stacks. Roadside viewpoints include one at Rainbow Rock, where nature has twisted beds of chert into an unusual formation.

Don't miss Harris Beach State Park (photos, pages 60-61), across from the state's Tourist Information Center at the north edge of Brookings. You'll note the deep sand here is a bit coarser and darker than in Northern Oregon. That's characteristic of the south coast, where streams drop more steeply to sea level and therefore carry larger sand particles to the ocean. Scenic rock outcroppings provide wind protection and climbing challenges. Many sea stacks rise offshore, including picturesque Hunchback Rock. Goat Island, a 21-acre sanctuary for migrant birds, is Oregon's largest coastal island.

You can picnic at tables above the beach, or on the sand between protective rock formations. Bathers enjoy both the surf and the shallow waters of Harris Creek. Fishermen cast off the beach for perch or drop lines from the rocks. A large campground is located nearly 200 feet above the Pacific on a bench once part of an ancient seabed. Open year-round, it has 65 tent sites, 51 sites with water and electricity and 34 more with full utilities; for reservations from mid-May to Labor Day, mail your request and $4 advance deposit to the park, Rt 2, Box 90, Brookings 97415

Drive through downtown Brookings, across the Chetco River to the town of Harbor, and down to the boat basin. About 850 commercial and sports fishing boats are moored here, near the usual tackle stores and fish processing plants. Forest products are loaded onto oceangoing barges, evidence of a $15 million per year local industry. Fishermen take ling cod, perch, sea bass and salmon off the jetty. You can camp at Sporthaven County Park, and enjoy surf bathing or surfing at the adjacent beach. The nearby Chetco Coast Guard Station offers guided tours, from 1-3 p.m. on weekdays and 1-4 p.m. on weekends.

The mouth of the Chetco offers fishermen an ideal avenue into the Pacific, one of the safest on the West Coast. Most coastal streams flow west, with their mouths fully exposed to ocean winds and swells. But the Chetco points south, its mouth shielded by the land from northerly winds. Brookings has become Oregon's sixth-ranking commercial fishing port, producing a variety of rock fish, shrimp, salmon, tuna and crab. Charter boats take sportsmen to sea from May to October for salmon and rock fish, and bottom fishing is possible year-round. The Chetco River also offers excellent salmon fishing in the fall and steelheading in the winter, plus good summer and fall angling for cutthroat trout.

Take a side trip up the north bank of the Chetco. Loeb State Park is located under a large grove of century-old myrtlewoods eight miles upstream. These distinctive hardwoods shade a campground with 53 improved sites and a nearby picnic area. Visitors enjoy beaches along the river, swimming and fishing.

Oregon's most accessible redwood grove is less than a mile beyond the park entrance. A hike of about a mile on the moderately steep hillside begins near a sign on the left side of the road. You'll see dozens of these stately giants (photo, page 62), relatively young

Above: The view south toward Chetco Point, along the Brookings oceanfront. Below: Beachgoers enjoy varied attractions at Harris Beach State Park.

ones 300 to 500 years old. (Not many of Oregon's few remaining redwoods are cut. One recent exception on private land measured 17 feet, 10 inches in diameter and 223 feet high; it produced about 48,500 board feet of lumber, enough to build a half-dozen houses of average size.

Little Redwood Campground, a popular place to camp, picnic, swim and fish, is another six miles up the river. The road continues 22 more miles to the edge of the 279 - square-mile Kalmiopsis Wilderness

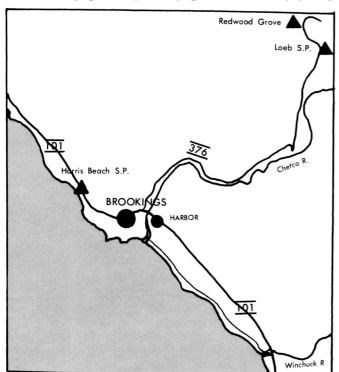

Above: Two girls admire a Brookings area lily field in gorgeous bloom. Below: Redwoods tower over a hiking trail, nine miles northeast of Brookings.

Area. It's a rugged area of deep canyons and unusual flora, including the rare Kalmiopsis, which resembles a dwarf rhododendron. The Chetco Ranger Station in Brookings has information about hiking trails in the wilderness and lower elevations, as well as about the redwoods and forest campgrounds.

There's an even larger stand of redwoods in the Wheeler Creek Research Natural Area, but it's harder to reach. You must drive 18 miles from Brookings, up the south bank of the Chetco River and then up Forest Road 4013. A short trail there leads to a spot where a submarine-launched Japanese aircraft dropped an incendiary bomb on Sept. 9, 1942.

The Brookings-Harbor area has a number of other attractions.

Native azaleas cover 36-acre Azalea State Park, at the eastern edge of Brookings. Some are more than 20 feet high and 300 years old. They wear pretty pastel pink blooms in spring, in time for the community's annual Azalea Festival each Memorial Day weekend. The park also has picnic facilities.

Visit Chetco Point, a scenic promontory on the Brookings oceanfront. Drive down Wharf Street (there were lumber docks here years ago), park by the sewage disposal plant, and walk out on the point. You'll be rewarded with marvelous views northwest past Harris Beach and east past large sea stacks and the mouth of the Chetco.

More than three-fourths of the nation's Easter lilies are grown south of Brookings. The fields bloom each July (photo, page 62) and the bulbs are harvested in late September and early October. Several growers of lilies, daffodils and other flowers welcome visitors. Drive out Oceanview Drive along the coast south of Harbor.

Other points of interest south of Brookings include Chetco Valley Museum. It's open Wednesday through Sunday from 12-5 in summer, and Friday through Sunday from 9-5 in winter. You'll notice Hastings Rock, which rises nearly 100 feet above Highway 101. It was a sea stack on the ocean floor perhaps 60,000 years ago. And you may want to drive up the Winchuck River, a popular stream with winter steelhead fishermen. There's a nice Forest Service campground eight miles up this pretty stream, which enters the ocean just north of the California state line.

For further information about this area, contact the Chamber of Commerce, P.O. Box 940, Brookings 97415, telephone 469-2213.

Farewell for Now ...

We've explored a marvelous land together, the most beautiful and varied coastline on the North American continent.

The sun drops below the western horizon here each evening, and gradually day turns to dusk and dusk to darkness. Similarly, our journey down the Oregon Coast must end for now.

I hope this book has helped you make the most of your visit to the Oregon Coast. May you have many opportunities to return, for there's too much to see and savor here in one trip.

I hope, too, that your visit has strengthened the realization that the Oregon Coast is ours to protect as well as to enjoy. Wise Oregonians, past and present, have staked the public's claim to the beaches and many nearby recreational lands. Their foresight has contributed greatly to our present enjoyment of the Oregon Coast. We must do no less for future generations — William L. Mainwaring.